The Effective Administrator

A Practical Approach to Problem Solving, Decision Making, and Campus Leadership

Donald E. Walker

The Effective Administrator

Jossey-Bass Publishers

San Francisco • Washington • London • 1979

THE EFFECTIVE ADMINISTRATOR
A Practical Approach to Problem Solving, Decision Making, and Campus Leadership
     by Donald E. Walker

Copyright © 1979 by: Jossey-Bass, Inc., Publishers
               433 California Street
               San Francisco, California 94104
                         &
               Jossey-Bass Limited
               28 Banner Street
               London EC1Y 8QE

Library of Congress Catalogue Card Number LC 78-24749

International Standard Book Number ISBN 0-87589-399-6

Manufactured in the United States of America

JACKET DESIGN BY WILLI BAUM

FIRST EDITION

Code 7902

*The Jossey-Bass Series
in Higher Education*

Preface

This book is addressed primarily to those who *need* to know how university administration works, rather than to those who *want* to know. That is, it is intended more for practitioners than for scholars. The dominant invisible reference group that I have sought to address—the tree full of owls that silently observe me in my secret consciousness—are experienced fellow presidents. In my mind's eye, seasoned and successful colleagues will read my notes about academic administration and say to themselves, "Yes, that's the way it is." In younger administrators, I hope the reaction will be, "That certainly makes sense. It gives me a feel for what it's all about. I see now how a great many things fit together that didn't seem to have much rhyme or reason before."

To this end, the book is pragmatic and, I hope, practical. The distinction between practicality and theory is not one of rigor or effort but of perspective and emphasis. I do not embrace the view that in the ultimate a distinction can be drawn between the practical and the theoretical, the immediate and the long-range perspective. But I do believe that theoretical and long-term views should inform the workaday dilemmas of administrators. Someone

once observed that true wisdom consists less in knowing what to
do in the ultimate than in knowing what to do next. Granting that
the two are inseparable, I nevertheless find that the translation of
"ultimate" into "next" is not always obvious in books on university
administration. I hope it is in this one.

This dearth of ideas useful to the practicing administrator
has several causes. For one thing, administrators who could write
books about the realities of university administration seldom do so.
In some cases they discover working principles of administration
but may think of them as idiosyncratic or trivial. As administrators,
most of us lack the proper lenses to see what we actually do. We
have no pattern in which to put our observations. The kinds of
helpful thoughts we might pass along to colleagues with conviction
seem like chip shots rather than long drives off the blue tees.

At the same time, the writing of theorists about administration often has the characteristics of unreal abstraction and rhetoric.
No scholar wants to be accused of producing a "cookbook" or of
merchandizing a bag of tricks. Their books thus too often enun-
ciate principles that appear in the abstract to be useful but for
which I can never seem to find a pertinent application. Their propositions are sterile of issue. What they have to do with the daily
difficulties of administration is unclear. The illustrations I use in
the book have been chosen in an effort to bridge this gap. They
are intended to supply a feeling of specificity. The transformation
I hope to work in the bosom of my administrative colleagues with
these examples is for them to be able to say, "Ah, yes, now I see
what the theorists mean." Thus my notes and illustrations are em-
pirical. They are drawn from examined experience, and they are
real, even when they are disguised or when they represent a combination of events and observations at more than one institution.
Their purpose is not to prove the point being made but to illustrate
it. As Yogi Berra once pointed out, "You can do a lot of observing
by just watching."

But there is more. The "watching" recorded in these pages
has been informed by a point of view, a frame of reference, a way
of seeing and interpreting experience. It is a cosmology or model
of effective administration and university life. This model is not
only optimistic about the administrative enterprise and about uni-

versities, it is more rational than most, including the model of campuses and the people associated with them that subconsciously dominates the perceptions of many administrators, faculty members, and the wider public. Moreover, I believe it yields better predictive results than others.

The application of an inappropriate model to administrative effort is the mother of cynicism and hostility. I know administrators who, although they have not yet succumbed to hypertension or ulcers, harbor secret thoughts that would poison a coyote. They complain bitterly of "the viciousness and pettiness of academic quarrels." Frequently they do everything with absolute correctness and "by the book," expressing bafflement when things turn out just the opposite of what they expected. I hope the following pages will provide a healing perspective for them. I hope also that this book will inspirit those who have become cynical about the administrative enterprise and who feel that in the garden of administration, the snake has the last word. Their cosmology, too, is wrong. I trust that mine offers an improvement even for such as these.

There are some principles set forth here for which I would go to the lions. Although I hold other views with conviction, I remain teachable. Some portion of these notes—a small part, I hope—will be what might be politely called organic fertilizer. I just don't know which part. It will be the task of knowledgeable colleagues to produce the necessary qualifications and refutations.

It is my conviction, however, that the general principles discussed here will be useful to most university administrators as they find their way through the "puzzle palace." Although my notes often imply or refer to public universities of moderate to large size—the kind of institution that encompasses about 80 percent of the action in higher education today—my experience with such institutions should be applicable elsewhere. There are differences, of course, in colleges and universities and the people in them. Large and small institutions have faintly different metabolisms. Those who serve "independent" institutions face problems different from those of professionals in the public sector. And graduate faculties are not the same as undergraduate faculties. But the commonalities of experience and the duplicative problems of administrators seem to me to outweigh the idiosyncrasies of circumstance; the philosophy and style of the most effective administrators described here can be taken, I am convinced, into the corners in arenas offered by every type of campus.

Some who have read these pages have been good enough to suggest that the observations contained herein have implications for the administration of organizations other than universities. A colleague in public administration has argued this view with me persuasively, but noninfluentially. The wider implications of the book, if any, for administrative amphitheatres other than campuses must, however, be explored and developed by people in those other areas of administrative practice. I have neither the credentials nor the inclination to do so.

Yet beyond my intended readership of university administrators, there is one group that I believe might profit from a volume such as this: college and university trustees. The marriage of power and innocence that is sometimes found in trustees can create problems. In the absence of an alternative perspective or cosmology, trustees may act on the basis of a hierarchical view of their institution and on what I call in later pages a "muscle" view of administration. They may believe that a roller-derby style of academic management is the only one suitably adapted to the kind of "standing insurrection," in Stephen Bailey's good phrase, that a university represents. I hope this is the kind of a book that presidents might be tempted to show to such trustees.

Finally, I am under considerable obligation to all the colleagues who march in invisible legions through these pages. In singling out some for special mention, I don't wish to diminish the implausible wonders others have revealed to me.

In my administrative apprenticeship, I was deeply influenced by Herbert C. Peiffer, Jr., a marvel of practical wisdom who showed me that administrative wit could coexist with unembroidered human decency. Daniel G. Aldrich, Jr., contributed in countless ways to whatever merit this book may possess. He perhaps most of all offered the lesson that the heart is a wise helmsman in administration and that all the theories are ultimately answerable not only to wisdom but also to humanity. I have also been significantly influenced by Ralph Prator, an infallible advocate of common sense. I learned much from observing Malcolm A. Love. And I owe a special debt of appreciation to a number of colleagues for their help, counsel, affection, support, sometimes their criticism, and often their forebearance. Harry Adams, Richard M. D. Childs, David Feldman, Richard M. Fontera, R. W. Gerard, George Gross, Darrell Holmes, Ned Joy, Adrian Kochanski, Robert Lawrence, Jack Little, Celestino Macedo, George H. Mayer, Major Morris, James Murphy, Ambrose Nichols, Jack Peltason, Mel Schubert, Lawrence Silverman, Richard C. Snyder, Paul Walker, Margery Warmer, and William Wild—all have a special place in, and a special responsibility for, these notes.

Daniel G. Aldrich III and David G. Brown have my deep gratitude for their complete reading of the manuscript and for perceptive and seminal suggestions. J. Victor Baldridge and Greg Stone have been especially generous and helpful. The detailed comments and editorial counsel they have supplied have improved immeasurably not only the wording but the organization of the manuscript. I owe much to Robert Morneau for unselfishly sharing his vast knowledge of the literature in public administration and for many helpful ideas. A special word of thanks is due Charles Fisher and Tom Stauffer of the American Council on Education for generously sharing administrative wisdom with me. And I must also thank James G. March, who, though he may not wish to be annexed to the views in these pages, nevertheless offered the prompting and encouragement that resulted in writing them. I owe an immense debt to the long-suffering people in the Office of the President at Southeastern Massachusetts University who have helped with the endless chores of preparing the manuscript: Evelyn Gifun, Marcia A. Gonsalves, Elaine L. Nevins, Eleanor G. Suesens, Catherine M. Sullivan, and Carol M. Vitone.

My obligation is less specific, but deepest, to members of my family for the contribution they have made to these notes. To my father, an academic administrator and author of deep wisdom, experience, and humanity, the debt is incalculable. His has often been the remembered voice that has made order inhabit confusion. My brother, Tom, a practiced and perceptive academic, with a keen wit, sharp tongue, and deep scholarly sensibilities, has often repaired the inadequacy of my perceptions. My mother, who has observed the academic community through the activities and antics of a husband and sons, has been an inspiring and steady influence. My son, Craig, by the wisdom of his questions and by his loyal skepticism has also improved the result of these pages. Most of all, and finally, my obligation for whatever merit is in these pages is deepest to my wife, Ann. She has been counselor and chaplain in ways that go well beyond the responsibilities of a loving spouse. I need hardly add that the appearance of the owl of Minerva in these pages has been conjured by dozens of colleagues. Regretfully, I am too exclusively responsible for whatever unsteadiness is apparent.

North Dartmouth, Massachusetts   DONALD E. WALKER
January 1979

Contents

      and Negotiation   134

Seven   Moving Beyond a Human Relations Approach   153

Eight   Answers to Common Anxieties   187

        References   196

        Index   203

The Author

DONALD E. WALKER, president of Southeastern Massachusetts University since 1972, has had a wide range of administrative and academic assignments. He was president of Idaho State University (1960–64) and acting president (1971–72) and vice-president for academic affairs at San Diego State University (1968–72). He served as vice-chancellor for Student Affairs (1966–68) at the University of California, Irvine, and as dean of students (1964–66) at Sonoma State College and at San Fernando Valley State, Northridge (1958–60). His academic appointments have included senior lecturer at the Graduate School of Administration at the University of California, Irvine (1967–68), professor of sociology and public administration (1968–71) San Diego State University, and professor of sociology (1964–66) at Sonoma State College; most of these assignments coincided with administrative appointments.

Walker earned his bachelor's degree (1943) summa cum laude at the University of Southern California, his master's degree (1947) in religion at the University of Southern California, and his doctoral degree (1954) in sociology at Stanford University. Walker is a licensed psychologist in the State of California. In 1973, the Honorary Doctor of Humanities degree was conferred on him by Southeastern Massachusetts University.

He is a member of many professional organizations, including the American Psychological Association and the American Association of University Administrators. In addition to frequent participation in institutes held by the American Council on Education to train administrators, Walker has served on the Commission on Leadership Development in Higher Education for that organization since 1976 and as a member (1971–73) and chairman (1972–73) of the Commission on Administrative Affairs of the American Council on Education.

Walker is coauthor of *Readings in American Public Opinion* (with E. E. Walker, J. A. Linquist, and R. D. Morey, 1968). He has also written for such journals as *Public Administration Review, The Journal of Counseling Psychology, The Educational Record,* and *The Journal of Personnel and Guidance.*

Walker and his wife, Ann, live in North Dartmouth, Massachusetts. He enjoys swimming, numismatics, and reading in such disparate fields as detective literature and medicine.

The Effective Administrator

*A Practical Approach to
Problem Solving, Decision Making,
and Campus Leadership*

One

———✦———

Characteristics of Effective and Ineffective Administrators

If the mother of the following ideas has been experience, the father has been puzzlement. For an academic going into university administration, the contrast between the rhetoric and the practice of administration is perplexing. Almost every new administrator senses that academic administration does not operate in the way it is perceived by "outsiders." Many new presidents are so struck with the new and uncharted character of their world that they resolve to keep a log of significant events. Usually their resolution has a short half-life. Within several weeks the log is quietly set aside and forgotten.

As a neophyte president, I too began, and abandoned, an administrative log. After twenty years' experience in several administrative positions, I adopted a different strategy. I still wanted

1

a better view of the administrative world and how it really works, so I simply began to drop notes about specific administrative experiences into a file. After a time, I took the notes out and recorded the regularities I had observed. I found that most of the notes dealt with two subjects: the behavior of administrators that I considered to be noticeably effective or ineffective and the way university communities behave. From these jottings, several hypotheses began to coalesce. And from the hypotheses, the following conclusions have emerged.

Ineffective and Effective Cosmologies

One realization I now entertain with growing conviction is that good administrators come in a wide variety of personalities and types. Because of the symbolic character of the office, presidents resemble one another superficially in that they look like presidents. (As my father, a one time college administrator himself, used to say, "Silver hair for a look of distinction; hemorrhoids for a look of concern.") But there similarities end. Good presidents can range in personality flavor from horseradish to creme de menthe.

A second and more important conclusion is that effective presidents tend to look at the administrative world in one way, while less effective chief executives seem identifiable by a different view of what that world is like. In contrasting these two groups, I admittedly present ideal types. No president of my acquaintance conforms entirely to either end of the continuum. Nonetheless, polar opposites in perspective seem possible. That of the less successful administrators emerged first and most recognizably from my observations and notes; only recently has that of effective administrators become clear.

Less Effective Administrators. As I have observed them, poor executives tend to be much taken with the status of their position and preoccupied with its authority and privileges. They often see the need to defend the sanctity of their office as a fundamental obligation, not necessarily on a personal basis, but because they regard themselves as inseparable from the status of the office. As they see it, maintaining the strength and prestige of that office is fundamental to the health of the university. Thus, they tend to react with threat and often counteraggressive behavior when un-

der attack. And because they seem to consider strong punitive behavior the best deterrent to future attack, they "go after" those who
"go after" them. They regard critics and opponents as "trouble-
makers" and commonly demean their motives and objectives. Protest and criticism are considered individual acts of malcontents who
might influence others to follow them if they are not resisted or
stopped.

These administrators also often believe that the heart of
their responsibilities is to make hard, unpopular decisions and then
to see that the derivative "orders" are obeyed and the rules enforced. They view decision making as a series of personal acts of
courage, will, and purpose. Decisions may be related to one another in that one decision might create the need for other hard
decisions; but they nevertheless view decision making as particularistic: Difficult problems requiring tough decisions come over
their desk one at a time. Administration is hence a process in which
individual will, ability, and vision confront unpopular but necessary decisions. This exercise of power validates the activities of the
administrator and justifies his existence.

The less effective group can be broadly characterized by
identifiable attitudes toward the university, as well as toward their
role and status. These relatively less successful executives tend to
regard the institution as either inert or perverse. They seem to see
themselves not only as the mind of the university but also as the
embodiment of its conscience. Part of the administrative task, as
they perceive it, is the obligation to oppose prevalent tendencies
to expediency, laziness, inertness, and other misbehavior. The role
of the chief executive, then, is to move the organization away from
indolence and mischief by enforcing a high and lofty minority vision of what the university should be.

Over a period of time, because faculty members and students entertain a different notion of leadership, their activities
come to be regarded by the administrator as perverse. Faculty
members are viewed as impractical when not seen as troublemak-
ers. The students are regarded as naive, mischievous, and easily
influenced to commit acts against the institution. Thus the university, in its corporate majesty, might be platonically incorruptible,
but unsatisfactory individuals gathered within its walls are the
source of perpetual deviltry. In effect these people are seen as es-

tablishing small kingdoms that have to be dominated; strong counter-activities are sometimes considered necessary for the greater good of a greater number.

More Effective Administrators. The characteristics of these executives became clear to me more slowly because the cultural lenses available tend to make the qualities of such pragmatists less visible. Often their distinguishing features are consistent and recognizable only with careful observation.

These people accept the privileges and status of their office, but wear them lightly. They separate themselves, as individuals, from their office. And thus although they willingly assume the ceremonial obligations and honors of the position, their egos are not bulky. Compared to their ineffective counterparts, the successful feel much more deeply that they are *primus inter pares.* They regard themselves as working with faculty colleagues who deserve respect as fellow professionals. From time to time, they may be annoyed with faculty members, and sometimes students, but the annoyance is always tempered with affection. They are not afraid of the faculty or the students. In a community of equals others' eccentricities are to be received with tolerance and good humor. There is no one who "doesn't count," from groundskeeper to dean.

In keeping with this attitude is their conception of the academic community as a group of legitimate constituencies with differing interests. Here, the rules of the game permit, if not actually encourage, challenges to administrative decision. Similarly, and perhaps because of this view, they do not perceive attacks coming from faculty or students—even intemperate attacks—as personal or as "threats to the crown." Their role as administrators is to work with and reconcile the differences among constituencies, if possible by arriving at solutions to problems. They avoid reprisals and have little or no need to punish opponents and critics.

The most effective administrators regard themselves as serving an enterprise larger than they. In their eyes, the university has a majesty and a kind of natural metabolism of its own. As an organization, the university becomes a reification that deserves respect. And thus the administrators are ministering to or serving rather than ruling. Metaphorically, they are not kings but elected leaders with constituencies to serve. With this view of administration as service, the best executives sometimes even consider themselves expendable if the welfare of the university should require that they be sacrificed.

Their administrative style is basically pragmatic. Since their job is to solve problems, they are always willing to accept alternate solutions, including, or even especially, solutions proposed by others. Reluctant to embrace irrevocable strategies, they regard their principal qualifications as wisdom and diplomacy rather than strength.

Finally, the most effective administrators I know seem to consider administration a process. For them, administrative events are related (often politically as well as in other ways), not discrete episodes or dramas. Not surprisingly, therefore, they tend to be "good politicians." They also have a sense of self-confidence about what they are doing; this characteristic helps them absorb the uncertainty of others and reduce the feeling of ambiguity in situations beset by multiple uncertainties. Their assurance apparently derives from an intuitive knowledge of the organization and appropriate administrative roles rather than from naked self-confidence in the egotistical sense. Clearly, they and their less effective colleagues perceive the university as organization quite differently. They see it as more organismic than static or perverse. And they have developed effective ways of moving through that world, solving problems as they move.

"Muscle" View of Administration

But what brings us to these conclusions? Why are not these obvious truths? Why are not these attitudes and behavior presented and defended by all experienced and effective administrators and with good warrant? Is the problem that, in spite of available institutional and administrative corpses, we do no autopsies? No. The problem is more subtle. It basically derives from a picture of the administrative world and its inhabitants that is covert and that many appear to entertain unaware. This conception hides the real world of administration from us. I call this the hierarchical view or, more picturesquely, the "muscle" view of administration. The outlines of the muscle cosmology go something like this. The trustees make the policy for the institution. The president carries it out as an enlightened despot (a cross between General Pershing and your grandmother). The deans and other administrators take orders literally and exactly from the president and carry them out without murmur. The professors leave the running of the institution to the president and the policy to the trustees. Their only concerns are their teaching and scholarly work and, of course, their students. The students are at the university to learn from those who know more than they. When the scenario is not played out according to this pattern, something is wrong. Pathology is present.

It's difficult to believe that such a view actually exists. It doesn't as a consciously embraced and openly defended perspective. Herein lies the problem. The reason for the potency of the position is that it is largely invisible. I have been challenged by fellow administrators: "But really, you're constructing a straw man. No one thinks like that anymore, either inside or outside the university." I counter that the clues to the existence of the cosmology are hard to detect, but they are there. In offering rebuttal, I usually need only to call to their remembrance conversations they have had on the telephone with irate donors or taxpayers which began, "How can you as president (or dean) countenance such views as those expressed by Professor Ramshackle at last week's meeting of the Rotary Club?" Or, "It would be far better for your fund-raising campaign if you forbade your professors to mow their grass on Wednesday afternoons at one o'clock." Or again, a telephone call that I once received: "I suggest that you forbid your professors to drive larger cars than the Governor's." Admittedly, the last is an extreme. But it's clear that the kind of world these callers envision is directed from the top, monolithic. Such complaints give an administrator a feeling of helplessness. To explain how a campus really works to persons such as these seems as impossible as explaining logarithms to an apricot.

But, then, how does one become aware that administrators too suffer from the same secret view that the administrative world is a pyramid with them at the pinnacle? One of the subtle signs is the barely suppressed desire to hoist the black flag and start cutting throats, to paraphrase H. L. Mencken. But the principal evidence that administrators also apply the wrong model to the university is found in the pandemic resentments of those who have these attitudes. They develop stereotypes of colleagues that are filled with black bile. "You know what that crazy son of a bitch did? He called me a liar." "She had the nerve to suggest that I didn't know what I was doing, and right in front of the entire faculty." People aren't supposed to talk to royalty that way, especially if the "royalty" derives its status from talent, hard work, and honest concern. Bragging to colleagues about how tough they are is a third indicator that a muscle view is operating. Sometimes, of course, the acceptance of the hierarchical cosmology is not at all hidden. An administrator will simply say, "I'm hired to run the place; I'm the best qualified to do it. Nothing would ever be accomplished if it were left up to those yoyos." But such statements are increasingly rare in these more sophisticated days.

The hierarchical-muscle view of a university has more than epidermal difficulties; it is full of bad karma for administrators. It encourages and masks a separation of the rhetoric and the practice of administration. Administrators operating under the unconscious impetus of this conception fool themselves. Writing about their administrative activities after the fact, they tend to see their actions in heroic terms. The personal qualities they list as required of administrators tend to be sloganistic. "A Boy Scout is thrifty, brave, obedient. . . ." "An administrator is strong, fair, decisive, purposeful. . . ." One feels that "only God can make a tree" would fit right in at the same level of abstraction. An administrator may say, for example, "I am paid to make the tough decisions. The buck has to stop somewhere. As far as I'm concerned, it stops right on my desk. Most consultation is just an attempt to avoid responsibility. Once I make a decision, I never change my mind. I just charge ahead and get the job done." Even when the rhetoric isn't quite that rectitudinous, the elevated tone is apparent. That same administrator, in actual behavior, apart from some blustering and posturing, may be noticeably consultative, willing to accept alternative strategies, and quite willing to share with others the blame for bad decisions—though not the credit for good ones. The contrast between the rhetoric and the practice feeds into a heroic view of the presidency.

Attempts to apply such a traditional hierarchical model to

the university inevitably result in the conclusion that there is much pathology in it. Such a conclusion then becomes a self-fulfilling prophecy. Chronic tendencies to confrontation between administrators and campus constituencies emerge. And eventually administrators pay a price in resentment created by the so-called pathologies with which they must deal continuously.

Democratic Political Model

I hope the foregoing discussion has made clear my central conviction that the most effective administrators perceive the university as operating, to a considerable degree, like a political, democratic community. I believe this view of university operation is a realistic one. Just as the best medicine presumes health in the patient, better administrative theory must presume that natural rather than pathological processes are at work in most of the phenomena of university life. It is an agendum of this book to establish a model that supplies a functional and positive interpretation of campus events as a substitute for pathological explanations. Not only will a more realistic model present a positive theoretical base from which administrators may see and describe their activities, it will also enable us to ask more nourishing questions about universities and the way they operate. In addition, a more realistic conception of academic administration will permit administrators to predict events more accurately and will contribute to more effective problem solving.

When questioned concerning his overall strategy in battle, General George A. Custer is said to have replied: "I ride to the sound of the guns." The gawdy fate of the general may not be visited upon administrators who, having no alternative plan, simply ride to the sound of cannon fire. But the embracing of such a strategy appears to reflect other qualities of mind. It was that same general who, on leaving his command at Fort Riley, Kansas, for the Little Big Horn, turned and left as his final instruction, "Don't change anything 'til I get back."

Two

Understanding the Peculiar Nature of Colleges and Universities

The writer's tribute to his friend and colleague came through with unreserved warmth: "The faculty had indeed picked one of their own—and a good one," he stated. "Colorful, irreverent, outspoken, Louie was a street-fighter in the ivory tower. And although his academic credentials as a scientist and researcher dripped with prestige, above all he was a free-wheeling, two-fisted humanitarian. The kids loved him. The oldtimers respected him." But it didn't last. As the writer, a fellow college president, explained (Davis, 1974, p. 24), this seemingly ideal president was being forced to resign. Apparently the faculty did not approve of his handling of a necessary dismissal of faculty members after a disastrous enrollment dip. The faculty wished its members to be let go on a "last-on, first-off" basis. The president disagreed. "I thought we should keep our best teachers, regardless of rank or tenure." Presumably he was to determine who were the best teachers. He acted accordingly and at the next faculty meeting received a vote of "no confidence."

This result was predictable. What astonishes me is that all parties to the encounter were not aware of the fact. If there is an issue at hand that the faculty cares deeply about and you can't persuade them, you certainly can't bulldoze them. That single principle of university administration is, in its omission, the source of more difficulties for presidents than any other. It is a principle that stems from a perspective of universities as pluralistic democracies. I don't believe those involved in the incident just related would have had the "Why me, Lord?" tone in their voices had they subscribed to this broader concept and all its implications.

Unfortunately, instead of seeing universities as pluralistic democracies, administrators frequently turn to other models in the society to make conscious or unconscious comparisons. Using these models, administrators regard universities variously as being similar to business organizations, to industrial enterprises, to the military, to churches, or even to families. In all cases, a hierarchical structure is implied. But in the real world, universities do not operate much like these other organizations. They operate like pluralistic democracies. This principle is sometimes raised to the level of conscious ideology but more frequently it simply functions as an unconscious set of assumptions like those held by the muscle-view subscribers. If this principle is understood, however, many of the behaviors of faculty members and students that otherwise seem to be merely random and perverse become comprehensible. Further, as I said earlier, the most effective administrators I have known sense the democratic character and persuasions of universities and incorporate this awareness into their administrative assumptions and styles.

The democratic political concept of campus behavior and perception has been noted by others, sometimes without great enthusiasm. The chancellor of a large system of public higher education had this to say: "Higher education during the past several years has been experiencing a tremendous drive on the part of many of its faculties to model educational institutions after the political state, with an approach to the separation of powers concept . . . Under this concept, faculties would decide on the mission of the institution and the curriculum to carry it out, and they would, in effect, elect their administrators and recall them when unsatisfactory, and all of this would be accomplished with the cumbersome machinery of participatory democracy and the one-man-one-vote principle, with large and complex committees assigned most of the decisions" (Dumke, 1973, p. 3). He concludes, "Aside from the fact that a campus is not a republic, and does not exist for the purpose of carrying out the will of its constituent populations, the political state concept of college governance simply does not provide for accountability" (p. 4).

Cohen and March (1974, p. 32) provide a less didactic description: "In the democratic model we picture the university as a community with an 'electorate' consisting of students, faculty, alumni, citizens, parents, or some subset of those groups. The distribution of formal participation in the electorate is the underlying power question. Members of the electorate choose the president of the university by some voting procedure, after which the president seeks to manage the institution in the name of the electorate."

Cohen and March extend the concept by talking about the securing of votes by a president, the promises of policy action, and the pleasing of constituents. Under the model, they stress the "rather elaborate performance of a brokerage function." Listing this as one of several styles of leadership, they too file a concern. "In the case of the democratic and collective bargaining models, the prime problems lie in the assumptions made with respect to the organization of public consent. The level of organization of faculty, students, alumni, workers, citizens, employers, etc., is essentially trivial relative to the requirements for efficiency"(p.36).

Dumke and Cohen and March use a more restricted definition of the political model than the one I have adopted. For example, Cohen and March stress the underuse of the "competitive market, anarchy, independent judiciary and plebiscitary autocracy models of governance in the universities." I include at least a portion of these models in the democratic political concept offered here. With some humility, but with considerable conviction, I propose that the political perspective has not been sufficiently explored as the basis on which we can make sound predictions concerning university behavior and, more than that, as the basis on which administrators can construct an effective style. As I have stated, this view is indeed accepted, at least semiconsciously, by the more effective on-campus administrators of my acquaintance and observation.

We can explore the pluralistic, democratic model further by considering four general operating characteristics of university communities:

1. The principle of the consent of the governed functions as an administrative imperative.
2. The pluralistic, democratic perspective imparts a moral quality to the behavior, including the decision-making behavior, of individuals within an academic community.
3. Administratively, universities have polycentric authority structures.
4. The foregoing characteristics predispose universities to accept democratic political procedures in transacting their affairs.

Consent of the Governed

At one level, it seems to be breaking a butterfly on the rack to devote time to a discussion of the principle of the consent of the governed. Almost everyone with administrative responsibilities seems to subscribe to the general dictum that all governance is ultimately with the consent of the governed. The statement is often accepted, however, as bromidic and with about the same level of conviction as "a dog is a man's best friend." Attempts to use the principle as an argument in decision making leave many administrators uncomfortable and push them into evasions, such as, "Of course, that's true, but then you have to be practical."

A trivial but poignant example of this principle is the problem of dog control on campus. One president who was having this trouble called her colleague at another institution that had the reputation of handling the issue briskly and without equivocation. "What are you doing about the dog problem? I hear you have a pretty good arrangement." The answer was "We have the toughest rules on the books that exist anywhere. We just don't bother to enforce them. Our policemen have instructions to chase all dogs but not to catch too many." When the students of a campus want animal control, a really effective system can be instituted; otherwise, it takes one policeman per student to keep up with the problem.

Actually, the consent-of-the-governed principle is a stronger imperative in the world in general, and in democratic societies specifically, than even "fuzzy-headed liberals" sometimes recognize. It has been reported that at one point in World War II, Adolf Hitler refused to ban silk stockings for women at a time of critical shortages for the Third Reich because of his fear of the concerted hostile reaction of German women. Those who doubt the operation of this principle should perhaps attend more closely and thoughtfully to newspaper reports of prison riots in which hard-bitten and experienced prison wardens, having sworn never to give an inch, are reported to have met with prisoners hat in hand and asked in one way or another, "Is there anything I can do for you, gentlemen?" I have even stumbled across an account which, if accurate, suggests that the principle of the consent of the governed may even have operated among pirates. According to the report, in June 1723, HMS *Greyhound* captured a pirate sloop, *Ranger,* off Long Island and brought the prize and the crew to Newport Harbor. The articles of agreement between the *Ranger* captain, Charles Harris, and the ship's company contained such items as, "He that shall be found guilty of striking or taking up any unlawful weapon, either aboard of a prize or aboard the Privateer, shall suffer what punishment the captain and the majority of the company shall think fit . . . . He that shall be found guilty of cowardice, in time of any engagement, shall suffer what punishment the captain and the majority of the company shall think fit . . . . If any jewels, gold or silver, is found on board a prize, to the value of a piece of eight, and the finder does not deliver it to the quartermaster, in 24 hours' time, he shall suffer what punishment the captain and majority of the company shall see fit" (*A Short History*).

Other misbehaviors are listed for which punishment is meted out jointly by the captain and the majority of the company. And the principle of the consent of the crew was also extended to some rudimentary form of group insurance benefit system: "He that hath the misfortune to lose any of his limbs, in the time of an engagement in the company's service, shall have the sum of 600

pieces of eight, and kept in the company as long as he pleases."
The agreement also provides, "Good quarters to be given when
craved." Whatever that last statement means, it sounds more egalitarian than pirate movies would suggest.

In their basic natures, universities are even more egalitarian
than pirate sloops, no pejorative comparisons intended. Apart
from common-sense observations and anecdotes, however, the
principle of the consent of the governed as a general fact of political life is suggested at a more sophisticated level by such statements as, "Even an old-style military dictator will pay some minimum of attention to what his subjects want in order to keep down
dangerous unrest." Or again, "A . . . channel of citizen influence
on policy making in authoritarian regimes has been through the
widespread acceptance by leaders of the *rule* that policies should
give citizens a good deal of what they want, even if citizens are not
allowed to participate directly in the making of policy" (Lindblom,
1968, p.44).

It is true that political scientists have observed great differences in tolerance levels among different groups for " authoritarian" leadership. A partial explanation for the seeming acceptance
of citizens in totalitarian states of what appears to be a high level
of despotism is offered by A. Lawrence Lowell (1938, p. 115):
"Civilization means cooperation, and is based upon mutual confidence. This cooperation did not depend upon governmental action
in the despotic Oriental empires because they interfered very little
with trade and domestic life. They exacted tribute, but in the main
the people carried on their affairs in their own hereditary way, and
their confidence was in one another and not in their rulers."

The wider applicability of the principle of the consent of the
governed need not detain us further at this point. Emphatically,
it operates as a general imperative in democratic societies and specifically within universities. There's a general feeling on campuses,
almost a religious conviction, that in a university people should be
consulted before decisions are made that will affect their lives. This
in turn is rooted in the assumption held also as almost scriptural
that a university is composed of equals. Added to these attitudes
is the ideology that turns around the rights of the member of the
academic profession as a scholar. These rights too are regarded as

inalienable. These influences make the consent of the governed an ineluctable circumstance of university life and behavior.

Consent and "Heroic" Presidential Action. The principle of the consent of the governed does not foreclose the possibility of heroic presidential action. It does not imply that a president never has the right to his own opinion or to exercise his option for splendid solitary and valiant undertakings. There may be times when the president must go down the path of righteousness like a thunderbolt. But in the real world, he or she simply does not have the right to delude himself or herself with frivolous notions of omnipotence when calculating the consequences of that course. If he chooses to act alone, he should recognize that in the final analysis, irrevocable and unilateral decisions on matters of grave concern to the academic community may well cost him his position or at least effectiveness. He may be willing to pay the price. I would only suggest that a president has no right, if he is truly willing to confront reality, to feel abused by this result and certainly not surprised by it. In truth, the presidency achieves its most effective if not its finest hour when diplomacy and political skill move the university, not when the president goes down in splendid defeat.

Some administrators reading these lines may be feeling a certain uneasiness at this point. "Now just a minute! Are you saying that all that leadership really can do is to count the hands? Are you saying that in the practice of the presidency, there is no really effective place for lofty vision and high principle?" Someone may even remember a statement by Walter Lippmann (1974, p. A–12). "The springs of greatness in a public man lie finally in the conviction that he must serve the truth and not opinion, that he must do what is right whether or not he is sure to succeed . . . this is the way of greatness. In the supreme moments of history, terms like duty, truth, justice and mercy—which in our torpid hours are tired words—become the measure of decision."

I wouldn't have the guts to disagree with that statement, even if I were inclined to do so. I am not. The subtleties of this point and related concerns are treated more completely in another chapter. I do feel it's necessary to emphasize, however, at the risk of being repetitious, that leadership in the real world of administration consists of full and equal partnership in the operation of the university. There's no room for unilateral command on most critical issues.

Of course, leaders must push. The most effective administrators of my acquaintance push with a sense of direction and extraordinary persistence. They do not hesitate to state their vision for the university and to do so repeatedly. They interpret events in the life of the university in keeping with this ideal. They negotiate skillfully and effectively. They use the established democratic procedures of the institution to the limit, with all the energy and vision they can command. Such administrators also, however, cherish deeply a vision of the way the campus should transact its business. They are mindful of the tone of decision making. They are sensitive to the esprit of the members of that academic community. And they recognize that in spite of vigorous forward thrust and drive, they do, indeed, serve with the consent of the governed. When they run contrary to the wishes of significant numbers of their constituents, they may persevere or try other alternatives. But when they sacrifice or modify their positions, they are not petulantly aggrieved because their lofty vision has been frustrated by academic midgets.

Beyond that, the best administrators I know are tutored by the recognition that they may be wrong and that if substantial numbers of their colleagues, faculty and staff members, and students disagree with them, probably they should carefully examine the position they have taken. They respect their colleagues in the deepest sense of that term, even when disagreeing with them. They respect not only the right to dissent but the wisdom of these colleagues, even when unalterably convinced that these same persons are wrong. Such administrators conduct their affairs with the realization that persuasion, diplomacy, perseverance, and a sense of direction are the most important tools at their disposal. They accept and use the principle of the consent of the governed as a positive principle.

I draw support for this general perspective of the campus presidency from the words of an influential and, in my view, realistic president of the nation, Harry Truman, who once answered the question "Is the presidency the most powerful office in the world?" by saying, "Oh, my, no. About the biggest power the pres-

ident has . . . is the power to persuade people to do what they
ought to do without having to be persuaded. There are a lot of
other powers written in the Constitution and given to the president, but it's that power to persuade people to do what they ought
to do anyway that's the biggest. And if the man who is president
doesn't understand that, if he thinks he's too big to do the necessary persuading, then he's in for big trouble, and so is the country"
(Miller, 1974, p. 16).

   Consent Versus Approval. In applying the principle of the consent of the governed, we must recognize that consent has both a
positive and a negative valence: consent for and dissent against.
The two may be thought of as operating somewhat independently.
For example, it may be possible to have a low level of consent for
a proposed course of action but at the same time a low level of
dissent. Many times in complex decisions that combination is the
most that can be hoped for. Low levels of dissent functionally can
translate into consent. For instance, the decision to expand the athletic program of the university may be received with somewhat
watery enthusiasm by the academic community, but there may be
no vigorous opposition.

   Consent may be contrasted with approval. The term *consent
of the governed* does not necessarily imply approval. The distinction
offers an important answer to those who object that they have seen
plenty of administrative actions taken that could not possibly have
been done with the consent of the governed, since no one was enthusiastic about them. An example may help clarify the point. An
East Coast university hired a tough, brilliant president with a reputation for acting quickly and usually unilaterally. Further, from
the description of the search and screen process, carried in a national magazine, it seemed apparent that the campus knew what
it was getting. Indeed, the search committee picked the new president not only for his brilliance but for his reputation for tough
and often high-handed decision making. I suggest that the campus
sensed, if you will, in its homeostatic wisdom, that budgets had to
be cut, programs terminated, and various kinds of "dead wood"
eliminated in order for the institution to survive the difficult financial circumstances already apparent and increasing. The new
president was hired to do the job of cutting. He did just what he

was hired to do. He did it crisply and in the style anticipated. People were understandably unhappy; even some of those who had given him the mandate were aggrieved. Consent, however, was present. Dissatisfaction never rose beyond some mutinous mumbling. But as the campus budgets came under control and most of the hard decisions had been made, the consent, which had never been accompanied by high levels of approval, began to be withdrawn. Two or three motions of no confidence in the president came forward from different segments of the university. How the matter will end is yet to be determined. Ultimately, the result may depend on the levels of consent the president can maintain in the face of dwindling levels of approval. Whatever the outcome, difficult decisions will be made. Universities are wiser and stronger than people give them credit for being. If university communities decide in their collective wisdom that tough and unpopular actions must be taken, somehow the job gets done. Parenthetically, I should add that tough, unpopular actions that are seen as necessary only by some outside agency or special enclave within the university will not necessarily be given this kind of consent.

The difference between consent and approval may further be illustrated by an incident reported to me by a fellow administrator. This dean had gone through a period of institutional strife and turmoil and had some dents in his fenders. Had the campus difficulties continued, he might have been asked to resign or done so voluntarily. But this period of strife had passed, and the performance of the dean was now viewed as improving at a fairly consistent rate. His consultative impulses were more active and his administrative skills applied with a softer hand. Then a setback occurred. There was considerable muttering among faculty members about the possibility of a vote of no confidence in the dean and his administration. After some maneuverings and discussion on the campus, the matter of the no-confidence vote was dropped, because as one disgruntled member of the faculty remarked, "We wouldn't have gotten 20 percent of the votes." The administrator in question later commented that the strategy of the dissidents had been misguided. The reason a vote of no confidence would not have carried was that there were a large number of new faculty members who did not know the dean well and would have hesitated to vote against him on a campus where no-confidence votes were not routine and not taken lightly. Nevertheless, the administrator commented, had there been a call for a vote of *confidence* in the administrator, that too would have failed, since the times were unhappy and since the new members of the faculty would probably have hesitated to express unreserved confidence in any administrator. An experienced city administrator and his wife sum up the difference between consent and approval beautifully. "Our governments really do depend on consent—not approval, consent. We don't have to ask for a vote on every issue. But we do have to know that any decision, any policy, any regime, can be overturned by the people out there. That's tough to live with when you've worked hard on something you believe in, but it is the price we pay for living in a democratic system. The veto power keeps the public administrator humble—an attitude much in the public interest" (Aleshire and Aleshire, 1976, pp. 312–313).*

There are probably a number of reasons why the inexorability of the principle of the consent of the governed on a university campus is sometimes missed by observers of university administration. There are also reasons why it appears to operate intermittently and sometimes without much rhyme or reason. The earlier illustration of the private university in fiscal difficulty reveals that university communities are more tolerant of seemingly high-handed administration when the university is faced with threats from inside or outside. Again, presidents can be exceedingly overbearing when their pronouncements have to do with areas that affect the life of the university very little. What these areas might be would vary from campus to campus. The continuing education program and its fate might be of little genuine interest to the faculty and students on one campus but a fighting issue on another. And so with intercollegiate athletics or a change in admissions policies. The president can also be very autocratic provided he or she is per-

*Reprinted from *Public Administration Review.* © 1976 by the American Society for Public Administration, 1225 Connecticut Avenue, N. W., Washington, D. C. All rights reserved.

ceived as being willing to back off should the campus begin to heat up. Faculty and students sense that in the final analysis he will be "reasonable" (talk hard and settle soft).

The willingness of academic communities to accept authoritarian leadership is greater when trust among the administrators, faculty members, and students is high. Relatively authoritarian styles will be accepted when other campus members feel that an administrator is making appropriate choices, and, bad as they are, that "He's paid to make those kinds of decisions."

A final word. Even among administrators who recognize the ultimate operation of the principle of the consent of the governed, there are some who regard the necessity to summon consent as an incubus. They argue that untrammeled administrative decision making is much more efficient. In arriving at such a conclusion, however, one may easily miss the fact that exorbitant amounts of administrative time are often spent trying to enforce commands and punish those who resist them when consent is not present. In the real world, sometimes "efficiency" can translate into a widespread, invisible underground of active resistance. That is a damned fool waste of time for everybody.

The Power of Old-Time Presidents. The principle of the consent of the governed as an imperative in university administration is seemingly indicted by the activities of the presidential "giant" of yesteryear. He was a cross between Billy Graham and a shark. He knew what he wanted, and he got it. He dominated his institution and the people in it. He never appeared before a student council to ask for advice or went grovelling to the legislature to beg for money. When he called a faculty meeting, as often as not it was to churn into rectitude the rascals who dared oppose him. At least this is the stereotype. The stereotype apparently is still alive, judging from occasional references at service club luncheons and stray comments of fellow university administrators over coffee. How else can one account for the frequent approving repetition of the supposed rule of thumb set down by Benjamin Jowett, old-time master of Balliol College: "Never retract, never explain. Get it done and let them howl."

The chancellor of a large system of public higher education, speaking of the days when higher education was less important to the society and when fewer people were involved, concludes: "Even in those years of low-key operation, the names that are remembered in the history of higher education are those of individuals who exerted strong leadership—Eliot of Harvard, Hutchins of Chicago, Sproul of California are examples—but in general, the issue was not drawn" (Dumke, 1973).

A former United States Commissioner of Education who is also a former university president and careful student of higher education comments: "Admittedly, the age of the autocrat, the day of the highly visible and often nearly omnipotent president, is over" (McGrath, 1967, p. 5).

I think there is a serious question, however, whether the omnipotent president of yesteryear ever existed other than in the imagination of outside observers. James March once made the observation that "strong" presidents always seemed to come out of prosperous times for a university and "weak" presidents always seemed to come out of bad times. Elsewhere in this book will be found quotations from William Rainey Harper and Robert Hutchins observing the limitations of presidential power. And Eliot of Harvard scarcely sounds like the talented tyrant of his latter-day reputation when he says, "A university is the last place in the world for a dictator. Learning is always republican. It has idols but not masters" (quoted in Knight, 1940, pp. 111-112).

On another occasion he expands the same theme: " The president of a university should never exercise an autocratic or one-man power. He should offer an inventing and animating force, and often a leader: but not a ruler or autocrat. His success will be due more to powers of exposition and persuasion, combined with persistent industry, than to any force of will or habit of command. Indeed, one-man power is always objectionable in a university, whether lodged in a president, secretary of the trustees, dean, or head of a department. In order to make progress of a durable sort, the president will have to possess his soul in patience" (Eliot, 1908, p. 238).

President L. Clark Seelye spoke in the same tone in an address at Rochester University in 1900: "One-man power is apt to enfeeble or to alienate those who are subject to it. In educational procedure it is better to lead than to drive. A heavier load can be moved and greater speed made, when all pull together. Successful autocrats are few" (quoted in Knight, 1940, p. 6).

Samuel P. Capen, of Buffalo, writes that the university "will admit of no tyrant anywhere within its walls. The relations existing between trustees and faculty and between faculty and students will be those of mutual confidence and respect; they will be cooperative relations in the conduct of an undertaking in which all are partners. Government, there must be, in a university or elsewhere . . . but . . . it will be government with the consent of the governed" (quoted in Knight, 1940, p. 116).

Where university presidents were indeed autocrats, it is probable that, high-handed as their pronouncements sound, these statements represented substantial consensus. For example: an ultimatum was accepted by the academic community from Nicholas Murray Butler at the 1917 commencement exercises at Columbia University: "This is the university's last and only warning to any among us, if such there be, who are not with whole heart and mind and strength committed to fight with us to make the world safe for democracy" (Hechinger, 1975, p. 50). Only a university president with a diseased fantasy life would deliver such an ultimatum today.

Nevertheless, it is perfectly reasonable to assume that university presidents did, indeed, exercise more authority in earlier days. Faculties and student bodies were more homogeneous and drawn from a narrower social spectrum. Teachers and learners shared a common body of aspirations and assumptions. And we mustn't forget how small colleges and universities once were. When Eliot became president of Harvard in 1869, the combined enrollment of Harvard College and the Lawrence Scientific School was 570 students. The University of Chicago had 428 undergraduates and 166 graduate students when William Rainey Harper organized the university in 1892. Gilman opened Johns Hopkins with 96 undergraduates and 148 graduate students (McGrath, 1967, p. 3).

There are other reasons to suppose that presidents may have exercised more authority in those days. For one thing, students enrolled in college at a younger age, and therefore campuses at least made greater pretensions of serving *in loco parentis*. Probably, however, a more important reason for the myth of presidential tyrants than past practice lies in the culture itself and in deeply rooted popular mythology. John Gardner, a shrewd observer of the American political scene, has stated: "The popular notion of top leadership is a fantasy of capricious power: the top man presses a button and something remarkable happens; he gives an order as the whim strikes him, and it is obeyed" (1965, p. 5).

Even those educational leaders who have no suspicions that the old-time presidential tyrant may be a fiction are at least persuaded that a new kind of leadership is needed. The Reverend Theodore Hesburgh has stated: "We are ready for a different kind of leadership. No longer must so much attention be focused on the president. If the American people have one overriding fault, it is the expectation that some man on a white horse is going to come along to lead us all across the Delaware"(1974, p. 36).

Moral Quality of Decision Making

The moral character of decision making in a university seems to derive from democratic ideology and the view of the university as a pluralistic democracy. When campus disruptions occur, they gain legitimacy from a seeming participation in this moral quality. Daniel Bell has recognized this: "We must realize that the issues of disruption and of the character of the university are one. The authority of the university is not a civil authority but a moral one. . . . Disruptive students can be contained only by a faculty and other students, not by the police. . . . This is not to say that police should never by used" (1971, p. 169).

At the heart of the moral vision of the university is the centrality of the individual. The belief that operates as a conscious and unconscious dynamic is that the individual celebrating his or her own intelligence through industry informed by moral vision will make the best contribution to the university and to the world. People are regarded as more important than procedures. It's not a bad formula. The formula was translated into operating procedure and style by one chancellor who insisted that if a policy was being instituted merely for administrative convenience rather than to benefit some group being "served" by the administration, then the policy would not be adopted. Needless to say, his was a popular administrative stance with most of the constituent groups of the campus. It felt morally right.

There are also implications for style in a stress on grass-roots problem solving. Again, the more the individual affected by a decision can be involved in that decision, the better it will "stick."

Decisions reached at the lowest possible level acquire added validity because there is a moral rightness about them. The recognition of the moral quality of the decision-making process in a university makes understandable many phenomena of campus life that are otherwise comprehensible only in terms of the belief that faculty members are crazy and students unreliable. To understand this moral force in the community, we might consider a term coined by Burton Clark: "normative bonding." Clark's discussion (1971) is largely peripheral to my immediate concerns, but his point is tangentially applicable. He suggests that to change practices within an institution, we must determine how best to alter the basic beliefs and perceptions of participants about the nature of the enterprise. He offers this as an alternative to the more common practice of changing the organizational structure. It is also an obvious alternative to the practice of changing administrative personnel.

The concept of normative bonding provides an important insight into the moral quality that is characteristic of university operation. Members of the academic community are bonded to it in part through their perceptions of this quality. This general characteristic has obvious implications for the political functioning of the academy, a topic for future discussion. It has implications also for the symbolic character of leadership. That is, the symbolic acceptance or rejection of leadership, and its general functioning, participates in this moral quality.

The entire matter of trust, discussed at greater length elsewhere in the book, likewise is related to the moral qualities imputed to and expected of the figures in whom trust is invested. This is a critical point for leaders to understand. One of the problems that authoritarian leaders have in universities involves others' subtle and pervasive feeling that somehow a moral imperative is being violated. The assumption that administration knows better what is right for people than the people themselves is resisted. Other ways in which the moral quality influences decisions could be listed, but perhaps the effects of this quality are most clearly illustrated in the "moral veto."

If 49 percent of the voting constituency in a university casts a ballot against something, while 51 percent favors it, an unsophisticated administrator might conclude that the debate is over. Wrong.

There is the *moral veto*. Just as the "consent of the governed" does not require a majority strongly in favor, so a veto does not necessarily mean a majority strongly against. The veto capability, based on moral authority, means that in an academic community any administrator must pay attention to vocal and principled opposition. Even though resistance comes from a minority, it is usually best to go back and do more homework, to talk with more groups, to present and hear arguments more fully, and to recognize that the long way around is the shortest. Principles have a special meaning in the university. If a person can argue with real feeling and conviction that what is being done is wrong in principle, especially if the argument is that the opposition case has not been fully heard, it's the rare academic community that will not stop and listen. The struggle for interpretation and credibility is then on. The problem will be negotiated as a political-moral issue rather than as an administrative or a statistical one. Let us say that a proposal comes before the university community to train the military officers of a nation suspected of totalitarianism. In defense of the proposal, someone argues that "at least we as a democratic society will have some influence on the future lives of the citizens of this nation if we offer such a program." A clear but not overwhelming majority of the faculty and student senates vote approval. But a group of strongly convinced members of the student body and the faculty oppose the action on moral grounds: "How can this university lend its support to the maintenance of a totalitarian regime?" There are demonstrations in the quad. The campus begins to heat up. The stage is set for a "holy war" because the moral veto has been exercised. If the problem is resolved in favor of the training program, it will be after a longer period of discussion and after more constituents feel that due process has been observed. The resolution of the issue will be political. Furthermore, in the final analysis, the political, democratic cosmology provides the best hope, perhaps the only hope, of constructive resolution, as many campus administrators have learned when confrontation has been pushed to the point of battle.

A final word. In spite of the perpetual possibility of the moral veto, it is an action that is always running against the tide. Unless a campus is very disorganized, it cannot be effective on every occasion. The prevailing ideology on campus is that most of the time and on most campuswide issues, majority opinion should prevail.

Polycentric Authority

Power is divided on a university campus. Honest, it really is. This is dramatically illustrated when students demonstrate that they have at least the apocalyptic capacity to "shut the joint down." It is strange that the division of authority should be celebrated as one of the principal strengths of the democratic society generally and yet be so frequently bemoaned in the organization of universities, not only by administrators and trustees but by people outside academia who simply can't understand why a university isn't run in a more businesslike manner.

Someone once observed that the real genius of American democracy and its most substantial contributions to the world were constitutionalism and federalism. By constitutionalism was meant the regularizing of the decision-making process, the establishment of procedures by which governmental affairs are removed from the whims and fancies of individuals, however noble they may be. Federalism was defined as the principle that decisions should be made at different levels in an organization. This dual gift has been bestowed in full measure on university communities. Whatever feelings we may have about the appropriateness of the gift, it is there. Here again, the best administrators tend to recognize the divided character of authority and power within the academy and to work creatively with the fact, rather than to complain about it and oppose it.

One factor that contributes to this divided character and predisposes the campus to accept shared decision making is the fact that the university is a reverse-discretion hierarchy. A perceptive trustee has observed: "The person with the most discretion in enforcement of the law is the patrolman on the beat. The same thing is true, of course, in higher education. The inviolate unit in which discretion is total is at the bottom. So we must have the understanding and cooperation and the initiative of people working at that level" (Enarson, 1975). The decentralized character of power in the university contributes to the effectiveness of strategies of coalition and also to a kind of balance-of-power logic as at least a component in the most effective administrative styles. (I will have more to say on this subject in the sections on the university as a political community and on style.)

Another reason for polycentric authority structures in universities is simply that academic communities, like the wider democratic society, have a deep distrust of concentrated power. This does not mean that influence and authority based on expertise are not respected. Indeed they are. In fact, they usually have great weight in the academy. But formal authority is something else. Community members feel that it should remain divided. Democratic procedures and structures are well received on campus because people intuitively recognize that such procedures allow decisions to be reached reasonably effectively and still maintain the division of power. "Now hold it," I hear someone saying. "If universities are so pragmatically democratic, what about the shouting down of speakers on campus? Is that democratic?" The answer is "No, of course not. Such antics are pathological and threaten the spirit of the university."

The rule of the mob in the quad as a distortion of the democratic ideal occurs, however, only sporadically and usually only in the form of an expression of the moral veto. The deep impulse that guides the use of democratic structures and procedures on the campus is the view that participation should be in proportion to the effect that the decision will have on the individual. The notion that everyone votes on everything, or at least everyone gathered in the quad at the moment, is basically alien to the most basic attitudes of the academy. The deep feelings on a campus support the structures and machinery of representative democracy. The emphasis, as I stated elsewhere, is on constituencies rather than individuals.

Handling Grievances. The view of the university as a pluralistic democracy, and the implementation of that view through the establishment of democratic procedures, provides a way in which disagreements that normally would be adjudicated on a highly personal basis may be settled impersonally. Disputes and grievances that become highly personal are destructive. The reasons why adversarial relationships tend to be so superheated and so unforgiving on a campus need not detain us here. Someone once remarked cynically that these antagonisms are exaggerated because the issues are so trivial. Suffice it to say that unstructured adversarial relations tend to drift toward becoming unforgivingly hostile and personal unless satisfactory resolution mechanisms are available. Also, catch-as-catch-can procedures lack authority and make it impossible to build "case law" to guide decision making in the future settling of grievances. The alternative to adequate procedures is a bad-guys-versus-good-guys cosmology. In properly functioning democratic systems, conflict and its resolution become institutionalized and more rational.

A word of warning is appropriate, however. The emphasis on procedure does not give license to make up new rules in the middle of the game. When this occurs, rules are quite properly regarded as tools of partisans. They cannot, under these conditions, be accepted as fair, just, and impersonal. As a result of problem incidents, rules can be made to handle future occasions. We cannot use them as a parachute for emergency situations. It is easy to fall into the trap unaware. For example, if we find ourselves starting to apply a rule that has been on the books but has not been enforced, we should take care that we are not starting to enforce the rule because it now applies to someone whom we dislike. It is very easy to rationalize, "We're not instituting a new rule. It's been there all the time. We are simply starting to apply it because the need has arisen," whereas actually it would not have occurred to us that there was a problem until some thorn in our paw reminded us. If, for instance, a rule has existed that faculty members may not give more than 20 percent of their time to outside employment, it not only looks suspicious, it is suspicious if the rule is suddenly enforced in the case of a faculty member who has been publicly critical of the administration while it has heretofore been ignored in the case of a dozen "hot ticket" faculty members.

The Value of a Constitution. Structures and procedures are not important, in my view, so much to enable the leader to work his will on the organization as to enable the organization to channel its opinions and focus its decisions effectively. They provide vehicles whereby representative democracy can be translated into the service of the "natural" inclinations and behavior of the organization. Accordingly, it is frequently helpful for a university to have some kind of document that serves as a constitution does to the wider democratic society. The document should be modifiable and adaptable to circumstance. It should provide for a division of powers and responsibilities. Such a document can create a climate for the campus, or at least encourage the creation of a climate, in which good and creative things can happen. The existence of agreed upon structures and procedures places a high value on compromise and emphasizes a pragmatic quality of decision making; a kind of check-and-balance system is encouraged, not unlike the national model. Such structures also assist mightily in the engineering of appropriate and acceptable levels of consent, as well as in resolving grievances. The style of administration implied in this discussion emphasizes the problem-solving orientation of all university constituencies. The procedures for such problem solving are critical. Merely good feelings, good will, and good intent are not enough.

Parenthetically, some of the alarm over the growing unionization of faculties might be mitigated if the contract with the faculty were drawn with a democratic cosmology in mind. As I have pointed out elsewhere (Walker, 1977e, pp. 60–66), the traditional industrial-union conflict model does not fit the academy. The constitutional model can be adapted to do so.

Democratic Procedures as Environment. Democratic styles, though well adapted to the character of universities, are improved by learning and practice. More than that, following the hypotheses of Berger and Luckmann (1966), we can reasonably assume that people of widely differing personality structures and predispositions can be socialized to the "world" of university reality, however a university comes to define that reality for itself.

I'm toying with the view that within organizations, certain kinds of "prepotent, predominating atmospheres" can be created which have an effect much like that of climate or economics or population on a country. This is not to say that other forces do not influence the university, only that when a democratic climate is established within a university, this atmosphere can have an impact on the university, the way it manages its problems, the way it adapts to changing circumstances and to challenges presented from inside and without. This point of view rescues administrators from the persuasion that their job is to remake people. Then effort shifts to the task of creating more hospitable environments for the expression of human potential.⌐

Leaders: Ancillary and Expendable

Because there is a feeling in universities that leadership derives its authority from the consent of the governed and is justified by its service to the ideals of the community and to the individuals within that community, universities regard leadership roles as basically ancillary. And thus the individuals occupying those roles are regarded as expendable. If this perspective is understood, it explains behavior and events that would otherwise be incomprehensible and the source of profitless resentment on the part of administrators. It is not a corrupt view. Harry Truman held precisely that attitude toward the national presidency. He was awed by the majesty and responsibilities of the office. At the same time, he was basically pleased by the thought that ordinary people could occupy the office and then be succeeded by others.

The President. Of course, the ordinary person whose expendability we are most concerned with here is the chief of the university. Later on I will make some extended observations about the ways in which presidents and other administrators are vulnerable and can be "bagged." But now I want to distinguish between vulnerability and expendability. It may be a fine distinction, but I think it is important. When a president leaves office, he or she sometimes issues a statement in which he declares that students, faculty members, and trustees have misbehaved so outrageously that his only honorable course is to resign. Occasionally, a departing president will state that the job was too tough for him or her. The assumption behind both statements is that a president leaves office either because the institution or because the president is diseased. After long and careful observation, I have come to the conclusion that presidential survival operates relatively independently of presidential competence and is nothing more than an accurate reflection of the political nature of the office and sometimes the institution (Walker, 1977c).

Behind the presidential complaints lies the assumption that a president should remain in his chair until he departs at a time of his own choosing and for reasons of his own. Another view is more realistic. When we interpret presidential tenure from the perspective of the political model, it becomes reasonable to assume not only that presidential tenure is limited but that limited terms for presidents are often healthy rather than pathological. Presidential exit can then be seen as a shift in the agenda of a dynamic and fundamentally healthy organization that is seeking an alternate symbol to give character and direction to that change. And there is a more subtle human reason why it is well to renew leadership in dynamic organizations. Over a period of time, a leader learns a great many things that cannot be done. But his replacement does not know what cannot be done, sails in, and many times finds that the old obstacles have disappeared or become surmountable.

Since the modern university has multiple functions and shifting responsibilities and since it has been among the most responsive of our major institutions to the changing priorities of society, it is likely to need different types of leaders from time to time. Probably no president could be the best leader for a university forever. In this regard, Richard Richardson (1975, p. 305) quotes Robert Lahti concerning a possible growth cycle in the development of community colleges, which, as we know, burgeoned rapidly in the '60s. Lahti observed that after four years, growth rates tended to level off and the institution entered a critical period in which it prepared to go forward or to decline. He felt that institutions that demonstrated a lack of control, management by crisis, an absence of subordinates prepared to take greater responsibility, and showed a lack of teamwork entered a period of decline and stagnation. Richardson believes that the concept may be applied beyond the two-year colleges. Others have observed, I am told, as I have the fact that senior college and university presidents tend to experience crisis in the fourth and seventh years in office. If this observation is correct, it may point to some natural rhythm in the developmental or operational cycle of institutions that makes changes desirable or necessary at intervals.

Whether Richardson and Lahti can ever be demonstrated to be correct or not is peripheral. I suspect that an administrative attitude that the organization is more important than the individual, together with a recognition that the best interests of the organization may be served by changing leadership occasionally, is healing. I don't mean to suggest that this state of affairs is inexorable. There are obvious reasons why presidents last longer in some institutions than others. When an institution is homogeneous and relatively stable, and when its major constituencies generally agree on its purposes, a president may serve effectively for a relatively long period. And presidents who are team players tend in my observation to have a better survival rate, since a team can shift its aims and its players to match situations. Presidents in large institutions stay longer than those in small institutions for reasons suggested elsewhere.

The many administrative talents and abilities that presidents bring to the office do count, but primarily as determinants of how effective they will be while in office. Survival is related to political skills and to institutional dynamics.

Ungrateful Democracies. Presidents who recognize and accept their precarious position in a democratic community are better able to deal with the apparent ingratitude of universities and to prepare realistically for their future. I've met a number of administrators who fight a rather chronic, subliminal sense of outrage at the "What have you done for us today?" attitude of faculty members and other constituent groups within the university. They complain to one another that presidents never seem to build up any credit balance of gratitude. Many a president upon taking office takes it for granted, for example, that if he decides to "hang up his track shoes," he will become a member of the academic faculty. He or she feels that the appointment will be conferred out of simple and uncontested justice. But when the time comes he sometimes finds that no department wants him, even departments that in his view were favored the most by his priorities and decisions. Understandably, the astonished and deeply injured president can only mutter to anyone who will listen ". . . and after all I've done for this institution!"

These presidents are using the wrong model. Admittedly, they are proceeding on "exchange" assumptions that are deeply rooted in culture: "I will do my best to meet the reasonable and fair demands of people in my job, and in exchange, I will be re-warded by having my reasonable and fair demands met when I surrender authority." But such administrators overlook the fact that most people do not like to feel indebted to another person. The faint taint of superiority emanating from the doer of a favor is detected and resented. Gratitude is not to be expected. The prob-lem is not psychological, however, so much as it is a matter of sep-arating administrative activities from the individual who performs them. People quite properly in democratic organizations view the actions of the president as separable from his person.

A president, then, if he cares about academic appointment, should make arrangements at the time he assumes the office, when such a proposal will be received, though grudgingly, as part of the deal. When placed on this basis, the future appointment is con-tractual and impersonal. The administrator who expects the acad-emy to react to him or her as an exception and on the basis of personal adulation is doing it a disservice. "But what do I say," I can hear colleagues asking, "to the member of the board or the faculty leader who answers my request for academic appointment with tenure by saying, 'It seems to me that's very insecure behavior to insist on tenure in an academic post when you are first ap-pointed president. Do you want to begin your presidency by giving that message to the academic community?'" The answer to that query could be, "I am exhibiting hard-headed realism, a quality that will serve me and the academic community well. Presidents are vulnerable, and they should be. I have seen too many presi-dents hang on to their jobs two or three years too long simply because they had no place else to go. That is unacceptable. My presidency at this institution will be a full and equal partnership with the board and the other constituencies of the academic com-munity. In order for me to play that full and vigorous role, I must belong to the 'go to hell' club on some occasions. The guarantee of an academic appointment with tenure confers that status on me."

The fact is, universities seldom make deep personal com-mitments to individuals, especially when such actions do not serve the needs of the institution. Even the naming of buildings after distinguished administrators often occurs when they are safely dead or at least departed—a circumstance which clearly indicates that institutional rather than individual needs are being met. In fact, a college's commitment to an administrator is more shallow than it may seem to that person. When a rock is dropped in a pool, the ripples subside very rapidly. I believe this is no cause for cynicism, but rather for hope. Universities can be concerned with people without making binding, personal, and extraterritorial commitments to particular individuals.

The Revolution Eats Its Children. Another illustration of the ancillary and expendable role of particular leaders in a university may be found in the high professional mortality rate of leaders in "third-sector" groups associated with the university. Theodore Levitt originally identified the third sector as made up of "those organizations [such as Common Cause] which have arisen to institutionalized activism in order to meet problems ignored by the other two sectors" [business and government] (McGill and Wooten, 1975, p. 444). More recently Levitt has spoken of a "new" third sector, which "seeks largely to change the institutions which cause the abrasions. It no longer seeks only to respond to the needs or problems of the dispossessed and ignored" (p. 445). Levitt feels that third-sector organizations have three things in common: first, the same purpose, "to do things business and government are either not doing, not doing well, or not doing often enough"; second, a reliance on voluntarism, "to provide the human resources necessary to accomplish the work of the organization"; and third, a common operating style, which he describes as "social or moral pressure used in support of the technology of persuasion by voluntarily associated members."

Third-sector groups on a campus—such as groups formed to investigate university investments, women's rights groups, and organizations to advance the interests of ethnic minorities—can be thoroughly annoying to administrators. Nevertheless, in my view, they provide stimulation from the periphery, which can be immensely helpful to a university in maintaining a tender growing edge responsive to the needs of the changing society. Maintaining effective leadership in such groups is sometimes a problem, however, as I noted above. Was it Danton or Robespierre who remarked that "the revolution eats its children"? It may well be that this cannibalism of leadership, characteristic of militant third-sector groups, derives more from their own nature than from the character of the university. But probably it arises from both. Though the problem seems to be less evident than it was in the late '60s and early '70s, it still exists. After leaders are chosen by third-sector groups, a process takes place in which the leadership group becomes increasingly sophisticated about university procedures. They become more moderate and interested in problem solving. As this occurs, the members begin to squint at their own leaders. There are mutterings about the leaders being coopted by the administration. Suddenly there is a palace revolution. The next week the administration is doing business with an entirely new group of leaders—back to ground zero. Whatever "concessions" have been made to the previous leadership are now regarded as history. A new set of demands is presented. The danger if such occurrences are repeated is that third-sector groups call forth protective counterreactions that can seriously hamper their effectiveness in the academic community. In my view, we serve the best interests of the university by keeping such groups effective.

My rather friendly attitude toward such groups derives from an interpretation of events in the larger society. I believe we are in a neo-Jacksonian revolution. Periodically in our history the dispossessed have demanded access to the benefits of the larger, affluent establishment. Sooner or later in a democratic society that demand is answered affirmatively. The gates are always opened more widely, and thus the base of participation in the benefits increases. Now, once more, the dispossessed are clamoring to be let in. I think in the patience of time this call, too, will be answered favorably.

The point for the present discussion is that individual leaders are regarded as expendable by university constituencies. This fact does have a real influence on administrative styles, perspectives, and problems.

Three

Mastering the Political Realities of the Campus

G. K. Chesterton once wrote, "This is the first principle of democracy: that the essential things in men are things they hold in common, not the things they hold separately. And the second principle is merely this: that the political instinct or desire is one of these things which they hold in common" (1909, p. 83). This statement could have been made about the university. I am not suggesting that all the behavior in a university may be explained in political terms. Nor am I suggesting tortuous and detailed parallels between the university and the organization of a political party, a political ward, or a political state. And finally, I am not suggesting that the political metaphor is the only one that is useful for understanding academic behavior. But I do feel that campuses behave as political communities to a far greater extent than has properly been explored and elaborated, even though the fact has been noticed.

My definition of the university as political is based upon the following observations. (1) The climate, spirit, and mood of prob-

36

lem solving and conflict resolution on campus tend to be heavily political. (2) On any campus people compete for scarce resources. (3) Underlying this competition is a basic assumption that all have an equal right to compete and to know at least generally the rules of the competition. (4) The fact that dialectic change strategies are frequently apparent results in an appreciation of the value of coalitions. (5) The end of the competition for resources is not the elimination of the competitor. (6) The right of each self-aware unit within the university to make its own decisions when other groups are not affected is generally respected and supported.

My comments on the university as a political community necessarily overlap to some degree what I said earlier about the university and its self-perception as a pluralistic democracy. I trust the overlapping will be illuminating rather than irritating. But before we explore my views, let's look at some others' remarks about the political quality of organizational behavior, specifically in the university.

Relevance of the Political Model

Woodrow Wilson is supposed to have commented once that he learned politics in the first half of his professional life as a member of the Princeton faculty; in the second half he practiced among the amateurs in Washington. Harlan Cleveland (1972) has expressed the view that a kind of political process is at work in the dispersion of power and authority in the governance of a university. And J. Victor Baldridge (1971) has offered a sophisticated and detailed analysis of the university from a political perspective. Although Baldridge's analysis is not as applied as mine and uses somewhat different categories and ideas, his book merits careful attention by those interested in a behavioral-science approach to these issues.

Closer to my own intention is that of Ann Scott, who argues "that institutions of higher education are as political in their internal workings as any other institutions but that their internal politics are generally more covert than overt; I shall argue that it is in the interests of management, faculty, and students to make that internal, political process (whatever process is used on a given campus) open and explicit" (1974). Scott continues by way of explanation: "No institution can be free from politics whenever individuals or groups vie for a decision-making power over the allocation of scarce resources. In the world of academe, scarce resources include such things as academic status, control over budget and personnel and students, the attention and time of the powerful. Getting published can be a political process. Getting tenure is a political process. Getting a larger share of line positions for your department, a new program funded, a course accepted as a prerequisite are all political processes. Deciding the ground rules under which decisions will be made is a political process. Politics in academe, as elsewhere, consists in exercising power, consolidating power, or effecting a change in power relationships—or, more crudely, in working the system to get what you need."

My purpose will be both more specific and more general than that of Scott. I do not intend to discuss in great detail, and in those specific terms, the distribution of scarce resources or the exercise of power on a university campus. I am more concerned with how the political character, impulses, and reactions of a university affect the way change takes place, problems are solved, and decisions are made. I am more concerned with the manner in which the political character of a campus influences the symbolic environment of the university, makes administrative positions somewhat symbolic and therefore vulnerable, and creates a cosmology in which criticism, properly perceived, can be constructively used by administrators. I will also examine such topics as the way the political climate makes communication critically important in an academic community. Still, ambitious as this undertaking may seem, it is less than that of John Rehfuss, who says that the primary emphasis of his book *Public Administration as a Political Process* "is to restore politics to center stage as the driving force behind most administrative behavior" (1973, p. vii).

Discomfort with Political Metaphor

Why do those discussing the political metaphor, as applied to the university, usually feel uncomfortable about it? Scott (1974), for example, refers to March and Cohen's use of the comparison as "odorous" but "not redolent of sulphur and brimstone." She also concludes a little defensively, "this is not the world of Machiavelli."

One reason is that in the past, the political metaphor has drawn fire from academics. It has seemed to them that such a description is a put-down and ignores the basic purposes of the university as stated in catalogues and general descriptions of the aims of university education. There is a teleological bias in the way academics see themselves. Ideally, the university is seen as an enterprise dedicated to the development, preservation, and transmission of knowledge. It is, or should be, dedicated to the intellectual enterprise, to things of the mind, to reason, to objectivity and impartiality. Somehow, therefore, describing the actual operation of the campus in terms different from these seems unfitting and disparaging.

But examining how universities operate as political communities is legitimately separable from considering the purposes of those organizations. Politics and political behavior are not necessarily corrupt or retrograde. After all, as Norman Cousins (1970) reminds us, "The big gift of the Founding Fathers to the American people was a political environment in which good things were likely to happen, not because political rulers might be benevolently inclined, but because the conditions were auspicious for creative urges . . . . beneath all that confusion were the energizing forces that would inevitably lead to progress." Joan Cook (1975, pp. 192) states even more directly her belief in the lofty nature of man's political impulses. "Man has evolved and flourished, not despite, but because of, his politics. He is a primate, of course, but a political primate; the first of all the animals to have discovered that his success depends not upon mere physical fitness but upon developing systems to insure the well-being of his whole group."

Although the basic impulse of these pages is not homiletic, I do believe that the political impulse in the academy can be raised to the level of awareness and translated into functional, democratic systems that operate effectively and carry with them all the strengths of such systems. By this I do not mean that a university must or should be operated like a New England town meeting. The processes are much more complicated than this. Administrators need a rationale with which to psychologically and perceptually handle the daily frustrations of their positions. From a broader perspective, it is the purpose of the university to serve the specialized and shifting needs of the society. But there is no tight market mechanism that regulates closely what a university does to satisfy these needs. The political process may provide a kind of substitute for such a mechanism.

Finally, if the ultimate aim of the educational system, as a whole, is to "form and maintain the political community" (Hutchins, 1974), then I believe it is time to take a more realistic and sunnier view of the political feelings and operations of the university campus.

Decisions Based on Bargaining

A university is, indeed, a community in which resources are scarce. These resources are usually distributed not in strict conformity to an overriding management philosophy but as a result of a kind of bargaining in which conflicting interests compete with one another and trades are made. Whatever the rhetoric, the value of compromise is clearly recognized in the way a university transacts its business. Compromise communicates a pragmatic flavor and improved quality to such decision making.

Subtleties of Bargaining. Sometimes it's a little difficult to detect a bargaining strategy in operation. The understandings involved may be almost intuitive on all sides. One experienced president described a situation where an action he took could have offended the faculty senate. He felt sure that because of certain other compensating actions he had taken, the faculty senate did not choose to take offense and acceded to his wishes.

The drama unfolded like this: A selection process was under way to choose a dean. The procedures, which were clearly spelled out and agreed to, called for the senate selection committee to present a slate of acceptable names to the president for his final choice. The committee presented a small slate but made it quite clear that only one name was really acceptable to them. Nevertheless, they left the door open for the president by including two additional names, one of which the president much preferred to the individual favored by the senate. At the same time that the selection process was going on, the senate was pushing two senior academics for full professor. Both men were popular with faculty colleagues. Both performed acceptably, but according to the stated and agreed upon qualifications for full professor, both men were underqualified. The president would have been well within his rights to refuse both nominations. The key members of the senate were fully aware of this fact. Semiconsciously, the president timed the announcement that he would make the offer of the deanship to one of the nonpreferred candidates to coincide with another decision—he also announced that the two faculty members up for promotion would be given full professorships.

I have heard perceptive presidents talk about balancing the good news with the bad news and presenting decisions that will be received by the faculty and students as fair tradeoffs. Even though people often seem somewhat unaware of the process, the political character of the university lends a certain validity to the strategy.

It appears to me that a kind of bartering, whether intuitive or explicit, was also apparent in the reports of an incident at a large university. A young Marxist sociologist was denied tenure by the department. The decision of the department was appealed by the professor. The appeal went through the usual university procedures. Meanwhile, feelings began to run high, and the campus divided. The matter finally came to the chancellor for a resolution. The chancellor awarded the complainant "a special fifteen-month appointment outside the department." The faculty member was not satisfied and charged the department had denied him reappointment because he was a Marxist and because of his involvement in certain reform groups. Members of the department countered that the scholarship of the professor was the only issue in the decision not to reappoint. The department also charged, however, that the individual "had engaged in a public campaign to vilify and discredit them."

Under the compromise appointment, the sociologist would report directly to the dean of the arts and sciences faculty and would not attend meetings of the sociology department. He was to be evaluated by a committee, composed of the dean and two sociologists appointed by the dean. The report in the *Chronicle of Higher Education* elaborated: "[the sociology department] will retain the right to evaluate [the professor] if it wishes. A hearing board convened for the purpose had absolved the department and the university administration of charges that they had denied reappointment for political reasons. They did, however, point to a 'flaw in procedures.' The fifteen-month contract was issued 'because that was the period in which a special universitywide faculty hearing board said [the professor] had not been fully informed by the sociology department about the standards against which he would be judged!" ("Pitt Reinstates . . .," 1977).

Feelings ran high. The professor in question was angry because in the decision he had been denied a three-year appointment. The department was resentful, feeling that the aggrieved professor should have had no further extension of his contract. The chancellor decided on the compromise because another choice would have required him to make a "pro-senate" or a "pro-department" choice. In the words of the chancellor: "The situation was potentially damaging to university governance. To overrule the hearing board would have undermined confidence in universitywide governance. Not to do so could have broken up the functioning of a strong department." The solution was symbolically sound. The chancellor did not appear to be choosing between two cherished and inviolable values, departmental autonomy and universitywide governance. The decision was "political" in the sense that a bargaining strategy, a dialectic compromise, was in evidence.

Tough Talk, Soft Acts. The bargaining and compromising tendencies of political communities, and particularly universities, are illustrated by the general rule that no one acts as tough as he talks. An example: A dean comes into the office of the president complaining of extraterritoriality on the part of another dean: "I have put up with all I can stand from that so-and-so. He's always out of his tree; he's always in my hair. I demand action. You're the president. If you don't get him straightened out, by God, I will." After listening to several more minutes of highly adrenalized denunciations and demands, the president says, "Fred, I like your fire. I think you make some excellent points. While you are still hot, I am going to ask Bob to step over so that you can state your grievances directly to him." The complaining dean objects with just a touch of alarm. "No, no. You don't need to do that. I am not sure I can be civil to the guy. I don't even want to see him." The president persists. "I think you should confront him, and right now, while you have a specific instance at hand and can make the point in your very effective and articulate way. Miss Smith, will you please buzz Dean Spread and ask him to join Dean Lynch and me for a minute?" Spread arrives. Lynch begins the threatened catechism. "Bob, the president and I were talking and I am afraid I got a little 'hot.' Well, maybe 'hot' is too strong a word. I don't want to make a big thing out of this. Maybe I am exaggerating a bit. Maybe I just have some wrong information, but I do wonder if you could arrange to. . . ." The de-escalation begins, the bargaining goes into operation, and we are on the way to a solution. Any president who would have accepted the assignment of being a go-between in that situation should be reminded of a Chinese proverb: "The go-between wears out a thousand sandals." This is not to say that a president may not, on occasion, wisely accept the role of intermediary, at least for the first round or two. The traps, however, are obvious and numerous.

The general tendencies of people in the academy to talk tougher behind a person's back than to his face on the way to bargained solutions deserve another illustration. In the gaudy days of student disruptions in the '60s, campuses often were brought to the brink of the abyss. Student demands came forward, frequently in unreasonable and irritating form. The trustees listened to a president's report on the situation and urged him on to combat. "We're behind you 100 percent. Don't let those snotty little bastards get away with a thing. You're a tough man and we're counting on you to show the iron that's in you. That's why we picked you. Call the police, call the National Guard, do anything you have to. This situation is simply intolerable and we will not put up with it." Some presidents were aware of the capacities of a campus for truly intemperate response to the point of ideological battle. They informed the trustees quite clearly that if they were to move with the heavy show of force and authority demanded, the campus would be noisy and the battering would go on for some time. Trustees often assured them that this would make no difference; they were willing to pay the price; the president should proceed. Many did. In most instances the trustees did hang firm for several days. With

suspicious regularity, however, when the trouble went on longer
than two or three weeks, the attitudes of trustees began to change.
The president began to hear murmurings of alarm and disap-
proval from the trustees. When the president reminded the trustees of their commitments and the ample warning of future events
they had received, he was usually given the reply, "I know we said
we'd support you, but we were counting on you to control the situation." Sometimes the denouement of the drama was that the
trustees began to bargain with the protestors on their own, even
to the point of calling for an investigation of the stewardship of
the president. The bargaining strategy was once more in evidence,
but this time with the president in a very bad position.

The point here is not that trustees in the '60s were villains
who wobbled under pressure. The point is that a president is ultimately tied to the results of misapprehensions about campus reality, whoever acts them out. The reality of bargaining and compromise is something a president should *really* know about and live
with.

Dialectic Change: The Role of Criticism

The bartering process merges into a strategy of dialectic
change. A thesis is proposed. There is an answering antithesis.
Often, or even usually, if properly managed, a creative synthesis
—frequently a compromise—results.

There is a notion among administrators that the quickest
way to get the faculty to decide what it does not want is for some
administrator to take a position on what should be done. This idea
is not necessarily a corrupt one. Many times, people decide what
they want by first deciding what they do not want. The process
delineates a natural role for administration as the initiator of
change in the academy. I am not arguing that such changes always,
or should, come from the administration, only that a clear and convincing role for administrators is available, from the perspective
of the political character of universities. This general principle of
dialectic, often proceeding as a bargaining strategy, is legitimate.
After all, other groups will be affected by what goes on. And therefore I see opposition and criticism as legitimate and appropriate
expressions of the political process, as the necessary antithesis in

the dialectic. Recognizing their legitimacy can do a great deal to mitigate feelings of resentment on the part of administrators. Even so, intemperate resistance and criticism are among the most onerous burdens that administrators must accept.

Accusation: A Fact of Life. A member of the administrative staff came into the president's office in a state of shock and indignation. He had been doing his best to describe a complicated series of events and misunderstandings to a secretary who felt disadvantaged by an action he had taken. The administrator in question prided himself, as an active churchman, on his reputation for integrity, honesty, and openness. So he was flabbergasted when he heard that the secretary had later called him a liar. The charge seemed completely irresponsible, as such charges often do. Yet it is the rare administrator who, sooner or later, will not be charged with being a liar by someone on some occasion.

This may well be the most bitter accusation that an administrator must bear, since most administrators regard themselves as honorable and do not subscribe to the view that the end justifies the means. Even those that might hold such an opinion would recognize that lying, being rather quickly detected on a university campus, is a self-defeating kind of activity. Very seldom have I heard an administrator, working closely every day with people, intentionally lie. The one or two instances I have actually perceived occurred in situations that generated great fear and personal threat for the people involved, usually coupled with the feeling that they were in a contest with ruthless and unscrupulous persons who would stop at nothing to get their own way. Even in these cases, the people "forced" to lie nearly always "confessed" within a short period of time. I believe it was Freud who once observed that confession oozes from our very pores.

William Rainey Harper, one of the old-time greats among university presidents, was regarded by contemporaries as a hard-driving and thick-skinned administrator and yet, in a paper written in 1904, Harper spends considerable time explaining why a president so frequently comes to be regarded as a liar.

> A superficial observer will find much to substantiate
> the very common accusation that the college president is
> professionally a prevaricator. Do not members of a college

faculty distinctly recall many occasions when the president
has promised promotion, or increase of salary, or a special
appropriation for books and equipment; promises that he
has forgotten as soon as the door was closed upon the in-
terview? Is it not true that on many occasions, students,
summoned to the president's office to meet charges made
against them, have left the office wholly satisfied that these
charges had been shown false and firmly convinced that the
president was on their side, only to find next day that the
verdict declared them guilty rather than innocent?

How often, too, it has happened that the president
in talking with one person, or group of persons, has seemed
to entertain a given opinion, whereas in conversation with
another person, or group, strangely enough a different
opinion on the same subject was expressed (in Knight,
1940, p. 7).

Harper goes on to explain that "the professor who thought he had
been promised promotion or an increase of salary . . . was received
courteously, and mistook courteous treatment for a business pledge.
The student mistook . . . silence for acquiescence in his own statement"(p. 8). Harper lists other reasons for misunderstanding and
concludes: "In all these cases, from the point of view of the other
man, he is, in the language of the street, a liar. And yet, I dare say,
he still supposes himself worthy of the confidence of his fellow-
creatures" (p. 8).

Sometimes the charges are more "serious" from a management and even legal point of view than being labeled a liar. A community magazine recounted allegations against a controversial
president of a large eastern university. One accusation was that the
president stole a silver place setting that belonged to the president's
mansion. The president, unruffled, is reported to have said to the
chairman of the board: "And it's either there, or the butler's stolen
it. So all we gotta do, we gotta call the butler and find out. And
let's just have him count it." The "silverware" (actually stainless
steel) was present and accounted for (Merton, 1977).

The fact that good and generally wise people are sometimes
given to such intemperate and inaccurate charges is subject to sev-

eral explanations, among them the need of people in a democratic society to find authority figures vulnerable. Authority figures stand as substitute parents, and many people are not fond of their fathers and mothers. Perhaps even deeper and darker psychoanalytic explanations could be summoned. But for our present purposes, the political metaphor is more useful.

Criticism is a fact of administrative life. It would be a callow and unsophisticated administrator who did not recognize this to be the case. Yet the desire to stamp out criticism has become almost a raging fever in some administrative echelons. Even the highest levels of government are not immune to the tendency. Nevertheless, the most effective administrators, however uncomfortable they may feel, resist the urge. Winston Churchill once observed with resignation and without apparent rancor, "We live under a constant drizzle of carping criticism." Woodrow Wilson, in 1887, suggested that administrators should "combine openness and vigor . . . with ready docility to all serious, well-sustained public criticism" (Cleveland, 1972, p. 120). Finally, Harry Truman made a comment about standing the heat or getting out of the kitchen that has become classic. The statement supports the same general point.

A more specific illustration may be helpful. A number of students, accompanied by a professor, called on an administrator, asking for a room to house laboratory animals. The campus was packed; all space was being used for some purpose. So the request was a difficult one to satisfy from that standpoint alone. But more significant was the provenance of the request. The psychology department, to which the faculty member and the students belonged, had already announced that, at this point in its development, it had no interest in pursuing animal studies. The department cited the expense of such studies and its own heavily humanistic orientation. Despite such attitudes, however, the department had proposed this faculty member, whose field was animal behavior, for appointment a year or two previously. The justification for the appointment was that students should have more exposure to experimental comparative psychology than the humanists in the department could provide. But since cooperative arrangements had already been made with a neighboring institution to provide space for the few experimental animals necessary for teaching purposes, it had been agreed by all that animal facilities would not be established at the university. The aggrieved professor's request a few months later, while perhaps predictable, was therefore disconcerting. Nevertheless, the administrator arranged for a small space in a campus laboratory to be set aside for animals. At the same time he suggested that the collection not be expanded until better planning could take place. The solution was unacceptable to the students and the faculty member. The next issue of the student newspaper contained a letter, signed by the students, charging the administration with a lack of cooperation, disinterest in research, and unwillingness to work out a solution to a reasonable problem. The letter carried the strong suggestion that promises had been made by the administration which had not been kept. Needless to say, the dean who had received the students and faculty member felt abused. The letter, of course, mentioned none of the background, did not refer to the understandings that the department had presented concerning animal research, and did not mention the proposed solution. From a personal point of view, the administrator's indignation was justified. But from a political perspective, the process was predictable and acceptable as a part of the dialectic.

I sense at this point some readers may be uncomfortable. "Wait a minute," I hear. "The department was obviously being unreasonable. Why bend at all?" The answer is that we are not in the business of punishing unreasonable people. As matters developed, there was an alternative adjustment possible that was more acceptable. Remember, as I will emphasize elsewhere, administrators are in place to solve problems, not to defend territories or to punish the wicked. And, again, let me offer the reminder that no one is a scoundrel in his own eyes.

Political Necessity of Immoderate Criticism. Violent and inaccurate attacks in an academic community, from otherwise temperate and accurate people, serve the same function that such criticism serves in the wider national political arena. It is an attempt to arouse emotion and to join others to a cause. A reasoned statement of disagreement or of aggrievement is not enough to accomplish that objective. People do not get indignant when someone reports to them, "There seems to be a misunderstanding," or "The president made a clumsy but honest mistake," or, worse still, "Things simply didn't come out the way I wanted them to. I believe I am partly responsible. I believe the president is partly responsible, but I may be mistaken." That kind of reporting is fine where feelings are not intense and the stakes are not high. It's a bit ho hum otherwise. For really getting the adrenalin pumping, accusing an administrator of being a liar is much more effective. After all, who doesn't dislike a liar? As someone has said, "People have a special kind of shrug for the perjurer."

It is to be expected, therefore, that if a campus organization is hunting for space and several alternatives proposed by the administration are unacceptable, the controversy will be taken to a wider community as a charge that "the administration has denied a reasonable request for space." Or again, "the administration is indifferent and high-handed. They are treating students shabbily." Such generalities will receive a more sympathetic audience than relating the actual situation, which might go something like this: "We want space for our organization. The four proposals of the administration don't suit us exactly. We want a corner office now assigned to a faculty member." Of course, we don't usually hear such complaints in detail. It is easier to build a cause on generalities. Whether such vague charges will have the desired effect and "correct" administrative decision or, in extreme cases, unseat the administrator, depends on factors perhaps best discussed in the chapter on the vulnerable administrator. Suffice it to say, at this point, that how seriously the charges or demands will be taken depends in part on the institutional ambience at the time they are brought forward.

No Heroes in Tough Times. The effect criticisms will have on an administrator also depends very much on the fortunes of the institution at the time the charges are raised and the context in which they are put forward. When things are generally going well, administrators are reasonably well thought of. Complaints will remain at the level of recreational bitching, with no latent demand for murder. But when the fortunes of an institution are bad, and continue to be bad for a considerable period, people personalize their frustrations. In the case of a state institution, it does no good and offers little satisfaction to a frustrated faculty to be angry with the governor and the legislature over the budget. That is like being angry at a boardinghouse. And so, although criticism may start with complaints about the stingy attitude of the executive or the legislature, these are soon supplemented by the view that if the president were really doing his job, things would be different. Ultimately, the blame comes home to roost. Of course, the sunny side of that proposition is that administrators get a fair share of credit, in good times, for events which may be equally beyond their control. Someone once remarked, "Who gets blamed for the rain may as well accept credit for the sunshine."

The human tendency to personalize frustration, to find a scapegoat to blame for the perplexities that make choices and action so difficult, has unfortunate consequences, as a gloomy editorial in *Change* magazine pointed out. "It is one of the tragedies of our time that we tend to see complex human events in the simple villainies of a few men. The world, of course, abounds in villains, but events are frequently moved by inexorable historical forces over which the immediate actors have only temporary and limited control. It is difficult enough to rationalize an irrational world, let alone account for it. So one is easily tempted toward the view that if only the villains of the piece were replaced by wiser and more honorable men, our worst quandaries would surely be ameliorated. And thus, it goes on in academic life as well. American academics— living practitioners, one would have supposed, of our twentieth-century revolution—suffer curiously enough from this same simplistic villain theory" ("The Carbondale Disease," 1974, p. 11).

Besides scapegoating and simplistic thinking, there are other tendencies that characterize criticizing behavior. For example, criticism tends to drift toward the top. Strongly critical remarks, directed at a department chairman one day, will include deans the next and ultimately will land on the president and perhaps the trustees. How far the drift goes depends on institutional chemistry.

Criticism also tends to move from general complaints about the nature of events and unfortunate circumstances to criticism of people, as well as from groups and organizations to individuals. Administratively, this means that the president or dean who heaves a sigh of relief because the campus newspaper takes a swipe at a department chairman, or even at the governor or the board of trustees, for some action that has offended it, should not become too comfortable. As often as not, the president or dean will appear somewhere on the list.

Responding to Attacks. As I said earlier, the most effective administrators recognize that criticism comes with the territory. They put it in some kind of functional frame of reference. One effective president I know argued in discussion that one of the real functions of administration is to absorb the hostility of faculty members that would otherwise be turned on colleagues. This president regarded himself as an object of blame necessary to the proper operation of the institution. Other presidents, while not so accepting, realize that criticism and attacks on leadership may fulfill a purpose. The right to criticize is, after all, a right which makes democratic governance ultimately responsible. At least it makes tyrannic leadership impossible. I do not mean to imply that everything that happens on campus should make us ruthlessly glad, but simply that in the long term, the right to protest, the right to dissent, the right of criticism, even extreme criticism, is justifiable, necessary, and, on balance, constructive in final result.

The political metaphor, as expressed in the dialectic model, provides as good a framework as any for accepting criticism and managing its psychological ravages. One additional advantage is that this model seems to provide a basis on which some of the more effective presidents can defend their detractors as a part of a loyal opposition needed to keep the administration honest and to keep problems in the forefront of attention where they can be solved.

Further, this model helps administrators look at the inevitable disagreements not as battles but as necessary elements in change.

Values of Criticism. The Persian kings killed the messengers who brought them bad news. The impulse is understandable, but a strategy of punishing critics is ineffective. It also tends to stop criticism from coming to the attention of the administrator, thus cutting off useful feedback on performance. One of the obvious values of receiving criticism freely and openly is the possibility, thus made available, of addressing injustice and misapplication of procedures. The grievance machinery of the institution can be immensely strengthened, complaints taken out of the underground and put in the open where they can be dealt with. True, the open reception of criticism creates a climate in which people feel free to complain, and do so. In time, however, the principal aim becomes not to stir up insurrection but to solve problems and, under the best of circumstances, to have a part in their solution. Finally, information about problems will be more accurate. The dialectic process is healthier when it moves on accurate information, although, again, the symbolic environment on the campus has a tremendous influence on how information will be received.

Importance of Communication

It is impossible to overestimate the importance of effective communication in a political environment and therefore its importance for the style of administration advocated in this book. Essential to that style is openness and full disclosure of information. What hurts administration most in an academic community is not what people know but what they do not know. The motto is "no secrets, no surprises, and no reprisals." Without such open communication, the credibility, trust, and understanding on which the metabolic style depends are difficult to achieve.

Some wag once remarked, "Confidential in a university means something that you discuss with one person at a time." Universities are whispering galleries. We don't really have any secrets worth keeping. Why try? Rather, we should emphasize efforts to share information and feelings about the agenda. In spite of the communicative character of universities, however, or perhaps because of it, problems with communication are legion.

Formal and Functional Communicators. One difficulty is defining exactly what constitutes effective communication. Like everything else, it is interpreted differently by different people. A natural division tends to develop, in feelings about communication, between what may be referred to as "formal" and "functional" communicators. Both are right from their own point of view. The formalist will say, for example, "Of course, the faculty has been communicated with. We advertised the meeting of the curriculum committee with a published agenda for three consecutive weeks. We even listed the agenda in the campus newspaper." If someone objects that "the actions the committee took will influence the entire campus and only two faculty members attended the committee meeting" or "a great many people don't read the campus newspaper," the formalist replies, "That doesn't matter. We can't be held responsible if people are lazy and inattentive. They had their chance. All the legal and technical requirements of the situation were discharged. The faculty and students have been communicated with completely as far as I'm concerned."

The functionalist, on the other hand, takes the position that moral judgments about what communication on a campus ought to be like merely confuse matters. Even if all the legal and technical requirements have been observed, if people have not been reached, they have not been reached. The reasons are unimportant—or peripheral. The functional communicator may then go outside established channels to see that de facto communication takes place. The most effective administrators of my acquaintance, while recognizing that the formalist approach has its points and that sometimes it must be taken, nevertheless tend overwhelmingly to be functional communicators. These people are more pragmatic than their formal colleagues.

Formal communicators sometimes extend their attitude toward communication to a misinterpretation of what constitutes a problem. For example, a formalist might be overheard to say, "That can't possibly be a problem. It was handled just right," ignoring the fact that the campus is buzzing over the situation. It does not matter whether a problem has a right to be a problem or not. It defines itself. If it's a problem for people, it is real, even though it's not a textbook case. Subscribing to formal communication as the preferred "norm" predisposes one to a type of administrative blindness identified by Rufus Miles (1969, p. 365): "The standard behavior—it might even be labeled a cardinal principle—of most members of the authority structures of institutions is to seek to understand people's grievances solely by what they say, and to expect the aggrieved to propose feasible alternative courses of action which will alleviate their grievances. If they have no such alternative courses of action, and can propose none, the administration tends often to think of itself as off the hook and to think of the alienated members as demonstrably unreasonable."

Individual Styles of Commnuncating. The most effective administrators seem to develop a feeling for people's styles of commu-
nicating, of truth telling and evasion. They are not judgmental
about these styles but simply recognize them and adjust to them.
The messenger communicates something of him or herself in spite
of all efforts to be neutral. This statement, of course, applies
equally to the receiver. There are different ways of hearing as well
as telling. It would be fairly easy to develop classifications of communicators, such as the helper, the snitch, the self-heroizer, the
salesman, the self-protector, and so on. Such lists are not too useful, but it is important for an administrator to understand individual styles in problem communication, for example. Does the
communicator tend to overstate or understate? The catastrophizer
frequently has exemplary motivation. He or she simply uses a reporting occasion to shed some of his or her own anxiety on the
listener. This is not a malady, by the way. The culture permits and
encourages constant informal exchanges of anxiety and reassur-
ance. "Do you think our budget will be finished in time?" "Yes, of
course it will. We're not that far behind schedule. But what really
worries me is another breakdown in the computer at grading
time." "I'm sure they've got that all ironed out by now. I don't think
there's anything to worry about." Unfortunately, catastrophizers
frequently go unappreciated. After all, who likes the bearer of bad
news? But if the administrator recognizes this tendency to overstate
a problem, the person bringing the news should at least get credit
for focusing attention on a marginal problem that might have
reached catastrophic proportions had it been allowed to fester un-
noted. The minimizer, in contrast, is a little more difficult to work
with. One has to listen very carefully. Potentially explosive problems are sometimes mentioned in such an offhand, low-key, non-
anxiety-producing way that they slip by. More will be said about
this in the section on incomplete disclosure.

Normal Embezzlement in Communication. I once heard of a
Saxon king who, at his banquet table, raised the question "What
is happening to my tax money?" His chief counselor, sitting by his
side, picked up a large chunk of ice, held it aloft for all to see, and
then passed it around the table. When it had been returned to his

hand, he held up the greatly diminished chunk. The same principle operates in communication. There is a progressive embezzlement of the original meaning as the message moves from person to person. There is distortion or augmentation. The principle of getting together managers from two or three levels to discuss problems or to receive instructions helps mitigate this process of attrition.

I have found that a rough rule of thumb is to allow for a 10 or 15 percent embezzlement of meaning in any conversation. Even the best-intentioned people, making a sincere effort to communicate, have problems. If husbands and wives who are emotionally close and earnestly trying to understand one another can arrange to meet on different corners of the shopping plaza, it is easy to understand the possibilities for miscommunication among the faculty, students, and staff members of a university. Where the motivation to understand is strong, problems may be kept to a minimum or simply brushed aside in new understandings. But where that motivation is weak, the loss of understanding can be frightening. Bear in mind, I'm not describing a game of cops and robbers. It is not a matter of wicked people and good people. The normal process of human interchange is fallible. For satisfactory communication to take place in universities, repetition is essential, summaries are critical, all legitimate avenues of communication should be embraced enthusiastically.

Principle of Interpretive Drift. Another aspect of the communications question involves the principle of interpretive drift. Books on administrative leadership often stress the importance of consultative decision making. The inference is sometimes drawn that once a decision has been democratically arrived at by all those who will be affected by it, then you're home free. That is only part of the story. After a decision has been made, agreed to, and promulgated, its meaning—its interpretation—begins to "drift." One reason may well be that many of the problems that reach an administrator's desk are ambiguous in character. Whether the decisions he makes about them are good or bad depends ultimately on whether people accept them as good or bad. Universities are full of bright people who would recognize and seize upon a good answer if it were available. When a problem lands in the office of a dean or a president, it may be because there are no good answers available. Often after the decision is reached, however democratically, the struggle over interpretation begins.

An illustration may help clarify the point. ʃThe time is the battered sixties. The place is a campus with a reputation for being conservative and calm. When protesting students stage a sit-in in the administration building, the institution is stunned by the sudden militancy and "insubordination" of a previously tame and mild-mannered student body. The full potential for holy war is present. The administration is presented with the "Berkeley invention," the joining of reasonable and unreasonable demands, all non-negotiable.* This is the climate in which negotiations begin. Word of the sit-in spreads rapidly. Within an hour or two, system headquarters is exerting great pressure for immediate hard-line actions that will probably polarize the campus and recreate the guerilla warfare that has raged on other campuses for months. The president, however, is able to stave off outside interference. At first, the majority on campus sides with the protesting students, although the tide gradually turns. After a few days, the vice-president calls together opinion leaders among the students, faculty and staff members, and administrators. By adroit personal diplomacy on the part of the vice-president and several talented administrative colleagues, all parties assemble with an agreed-upon plan for problem-solving. The group is to stay together for a marathon session, even though it may take several days and nights to resolve the critical issues. Whatever agreements are reached will be referred to appropriate faculty and student decision-making bodies for discussion and, if all goes well, ratification. The fact that

*The "Berkeley invention" consists of demands such as these: (1) Additional students on several major university committees. (Reasonable.) (2) The right of students to vote on whether an ROTC unit should remain on campus. (Perhaps reasonable. The faculty should be involved also. The nature of the contract should be examined. The proposition requires much more study.) (3) The contract of a nontenured controversial professor to be renewed. (Perhaps reasonable. It depends on how the individual fares in the campus process of recommendation and how a grievance filed against him by students on a charge of intimidating students is resolved.) (4) The United States to withdraw from the Vietnam War by the following Thursday.

such a disparate group of leaders as that represented in the task force could arrive at an agreement will presumably lend the proposals great credibility with all reviewing bodies. After a day and a half of discussion in which several individuals demonstrate truly remarkable group leadership, a series of agreements is reached. The agreements do not violate the procedures or the standards of the university but offer reasonable and necessary concessions to the protesting students. The agreements reached will be popular with the moderate student leadership and with the leaders of the faculty. The unbelievable has occurred. All parties are euphoric about the results. The accolades pour in: "A new day for the university." "A new spirit of accord and team effort." "A truly brilliant example of university problem-solving at a time when repeated disruptions were virtually destroying other campuses." "Convincing evidence that the university working as a community can solve its own problems." As an added bonus, the agreements have been reached within the time limits that most off-campus authorities accepted as generally reasonable. The attorney from system headquarters assigned to the campus is pleased and announces, the evening the agreement is reached, that he has never seen a campus disruption handled so efficiently, so constructively for all concerned and with such a reasonable outcome. What could be better! The next day, the faculty coffee room is abuzz with praise for the administrator who is regarded as the principal architect of the "victory." The compromise solution is the wisest and best that has ever come from administrative echelons. So much for the first round.

Several days later, while approval is still being voiced, but with diminishing frenzy, one faculty member is heard to remark, "Yes, that was a great job of bringing people together—would you say slick?" Within two weeks, the administration is vigorously struggling for credibility in the face of charges concerning "the slickest job of co-opting this institution that has ever been pulled off." The principle of interpretive drift is in operation.

The implications of this story for administration are that it is not enough to make decisions well, carefully, and consultatively. The moment difficult decisions are made, another process must begin. They must be interpreted and "marketed." It is never "obvious" that difficult decisions are the right ones.

Another example of interpretive drift may be helpful. The governor of the state has come to the campus. The students have packed the auditorium in an angry, and sometimes raucous, mood to ask the governor to approve a bill providing for the state to "take over" the student center in order to cut student fees. Since the campus center had been built several years before without administrative or legislative approval, the legislature and governor had been cool to the notion that the state should assume the obligation. Feelings were on the mend, however.

The governor conducts an articulate, long, and sometimes heated discussion with the assembled students. He appears to be hunting for some sort of equitable solution to the situation. Finally, the governor proposes, apparently spontaneously, that if the students will agree to a modest increase in tuition, he will sign the bill providing for the state to take over the center. He is roundly cheered for his proposal. Acceptance of the idea seems unanimous. Not a dissenting voice is raised in the vast auditorium. It is assumed that the tuition proposal will go over all the "jumps" without much opposition.

The week after the meeting with the governor, the student council meets and the student trustee who has so spiritedly and effectively presented the student case before the governor in the auditorium is already something of a villain. "A small but vocal minority" of students are saying that a "deal" was made with the governor before the meeting and that the student trustee was the willing dupe of the governor in forcing increased tuition on students. By this time, considerable numbers of students are convinced that, indeed, the charges have considerable merit. As it develops, the discontent is finally meliorated somewhat in the dialectic process. The student newspaper defends the "deal" as fair and openly arrived at. The point, however, is that decisions are not self-validating. The initial interpretations tend to change.

Explaining and Owning Problems. Another characteristic of the communications process is that the person who explains the problem owns the problem. For instance a university administrator was assigned to act as the liaison with the food service company with which the university had signed a contract. After several months of mounting dissatisfaction with the quality and quantity of the meals served, students complained to the administrator. But instead of arranging for the students to talk with officials of the food service, he began explaining the company's problems. The price of help was increasing, the price of food was going up, good chefs were hard to find and to keep. . . . Before long, student delegations were talking to the president, demanding that the administrator be fired, even though he had nothing to do with the making of menus or the pricing policy. Explanations that the administrator was not, in fact, in any way involved in the food service, except as a liaison, did not sell, because by defending the service, he had come to represent the company and therefore to symbolize the source of the problem. The refusal to dismiss the administrator created considerable problems for some time. If someone explains a problem long enough and often enough, that person winds up owning the problem. It is important, in establishing administrative problem-solving plans, to recognize this fact. It may mean that the person most able to remedy a problem should receive complaints. Sometimes it also means that the responsibility for communication belongs to everyone and should be widely shared.

Art of Incomplete Disclosure. I believe it was Harold W. Stoke in his book on *The American College President* (1959) who first used the term "the art of incomplete disclosure." As I recall, he was pessimistic about a cure for the disease. The practitioner of the art does not burden the inquirer with superfluous information lest it unsettle the judgment, even though it is obvious what information is being sought. If just precisely the right button is not pushed, the information doesn't come forward. I've heard presidents observe that, in their opinion, business officers are much given to this malady. That may be true, but I do not subscribe to the view that business officers are uniquely susceptible to the affliction.

One advantage of team administration (whose other benefits are described later) is that eventually the chronic tendency to "hold out" is noticed. It is the rare piece of critical information that is not available to more than one person in a group, at least to the degree that intelligent questions can be asked. Repair is possible. In the administrative style I am talking about, a kind of informal "Sunshine Law" is in operation. All books are open and available for inspection by anyone. Practicing the short-changing art in communication is difficult under such conditions.

Another form of incomplete disclosure is to deliver unwelcome news in an offhand manner, without the cultural flags usually flown to get attention. The news may be mentioned casually at the end of a long series of items or presented in highly cosmetic and nondisturbing language. Later, regrettably, when called to account, the reporter is likely to say, fully convinced of the complete accuracy of the defense, "Oh! I gave the president information about that problem two weeks ago on such and such a date." Whereas such embezzlement is normal and human, it is sometimes the source of problems.

Finally, there is another type of incomplete delivery that can be especially maddening to hard-pressed administrators. This is the refusal of the provider to give the information in the form that's requested. He presents information related to the problem but usually with a modifying phrase: "I know you asked for the information in a particular way. But I don't think you really want the data in that form. I've given it to you in a somewhat different way. Let me explain." Usually the administrator requesting the information has reasons for wanting it in a particular form. The seeming evasion, however well-intentioned, is frustrating. The problem is merely annoying if the keeper of the data can successfully be sent back to return with the facts in the preferred form. It's amazing, however, how often data constables seem to feel that the facts and figures must be protected from administrative molesters who might misuse the information. Since the data base in a university is usually accessible to almost anyone, one cure is to simply send someone else after the data.

Intemperate Memoranda. Universities, because they are political communities, seem peculiarly susceptible to occasional attacks of immoderate memoranda. A case in point: Budget cuts threaten an institution. The budget review committee recommends that for the next year all vacant positions be filled with part-time people, since a good supply of well-trained professionals is available in the local community. The committee reasons that if budget cuts are, indeed, visited upon the institution, the dismissal of part-time people would be relatively less traumatic for the university than the release of full-time people. One department objects. Its members feel that they have more than their share of vacancies for the year. They insist on full-time appointments. Excited meetings are held.

Students are invited into the excitement. The minutes of meetings are widely circulated; charges are made that the administration has as its real objective the dismantling of the department. Worried students come to see the dean. The dean reviews with them the information leading up to the decision to hire part-time people, pointing out that the department in question is being treated no differently from any other department. The message somehow doesn't get through.

Finally the department frames a set of resolutions directed to the administration and sends them to the student newspaper. The demands of the department are these: (1) Full-time faculty positions must be released to the department immediately. (2) If the administration should fail to comply with this demand, then every administrator, including the president, should teach one or two courses in his or her academic specialty. Fewer part-timers will need to be hired, and thus there will be enough money for more full-time faculty members in the department in question. (3) The administration must apologize to the majors of the department for seriously damaging the morale of the department. (4) As an alternative, all administrators are to voluntarily accept a cut in pay, the money to be used to hire full-time faculty members for the department. The memorandum is irritating and threatening, as it is intended to be.

An administrator drafts a reply to be sent to the department, with a copy to the student newspaper, pointing out that the department in question has the lowest teaching loads in the university and that many members of the department have poor publications and university-service records. The administrator also advances some counterproposals: (1) All members of the department are to raise their teaching loads to the average of the university. This will mean at least one more course for most members of the department. (2) Every member of the department who has not published at least one article in the past two years must teach an overload. (3) The department is to apologize to the administration and to the student body for disseminating misinformation and spreading rumors in a budget crisis.

Of course the memorandum was not sent. But there is always the perfectly normal tendency for administrators to join in a progressive escalation of memos. Such activity can only compound the confusion.

Faculty members suffer from rather chronic feelings of interference, harassment, and restraint from administrators. Too often, they also feel helpless. It is not surprising, then, that intemperate memoranda come forward with some regularity from the more articulate and choleric members of the faculty. Not infrequently, these memoranda are based on misunderstandings and misinformation. The administrator is naturally tempted to demonstrate that he or she is just as articulate and can be just as splenetic as the accuser. Furthermore, he gets his need to "set the record straight" confused with his feelings of moral outrage at the unjust accusation. So he succumbs to the urge to fire back a more wittily sarcastic reply. The action escalates. The entire operation is simply bad news.

Administrators should recognize that a part of their role is to absorb the hostility and misunderstandings of others. If a factual reply is required, then the memorandum should be short, without any hint of rancor or outrage, and should, of course, be totally devoid of sarcasm. Usually, it is better not to reply in writing at all, but simply to phone the sender and explain or, better yet, to drop into his or her office for a conversation. After the correct information is supplied, assuming it is accepted, a discreet inquiry about whether or not it would be helpful to clear up the record with colleagues may be productive. If not, forget it. In any event, when a president sees fellow administrators and faculty members beginning to sail paper airplanes at one another, he should call the administrative team in and invite them to "feel free not to do that."

Sharing Information. The press is as vital to the communication process of a university as it is to any political organization or agency. One of the too frequently neglected agencies of potentially effective communication on the campus is the campus newspaper. It is one of the most important "constituencies" of a president or, indeed, of any administrator. In my opinion, there is no better way to keep close to a campus newspaper than to meet regularly with its staff. How effective these meetings will be depends on the attitude with which they are conducted. The important thing is to build a relationship of trust, complete openness, and honesty. If the newspaper staff senses a demand for blind support, you're out of business. There are hazards, of course. I think the hazards are worth the risk. Just to demonstrate its independence, the newspaper will almost be required to give the administration a hot foot a few times each year. And no administrator should expect immunity when the press, campus or otherwise, comes upon embarrassing information.

The same approach can be used with the off-campus press. Several good presidents I know have discovered that a press luncheon, held once every two weeks when campus events are pressing, once a month or every six weeks when the campus is relatively serene, can be immensely rewarding in terms of improved understanding. A few presidents use the press briefing to be completely candid. The only understanding is that no direct quotations are to come from such a briefing. One administrator explained the rule by saying, "I want to be free to snort, wave my arms, and be metaphorical in my statements. I would not like to see casual or colloquial phrases come back to me the next day in the alienated majesty of the printed page." All topics are fair game, but the reporter should simply step forward after the press briefing and say, "I'd like to do a story on that topic. Will you give me something for quoting?" If the press agrees to these arrangements, the plan works well. All participants should clearly understand the ground rules, however, before the meeting begins. The president is acting unfairly if he or she talks for fifteen minutes on a hot topic, and then says "By the way, this is off the record." In fact, I have found the press to be extraordinarily sensitive to that statement. It should not be used unless it is absolutely necessary and laid down in the ground rules, as just indicated. Often the administrator is wise to leave it out and take his chances. The observation bears repetition that the secret ingredients are trust and credibility. Giving accurate information is essential to building such attitudes.

Sometimes institutions have supplemented the campus newspaper by putting out either an administrative page in the student newspaper or an "independent" newspaper. This practice has been followed by some rather prestigious schools with good reputations for fairness and objectivity. How successful the effort will be depends on how unbiased the publication is and is perceived to be. If it is seen as just an administrative rag, it's probably not worth the effort. If all the facts are printed fully and fairly and without evasion, even when they are embarrassing to the administration, the result can be very helpful and constructive.

Shortening up the lines by arranging face-to-face communication sessions with opinion leaders in the university also can be immensely useful. Sometimes it is a little difficult to rationalize such meetings from the standpoint of the published organization charts. But such gatherings can be helpful provided the participants clearly understand that they are called together not to make decisions but to improve communication and perspective and, informally, to advise the president.

A final thought on this general theme: attempts to hide damaging bits of information or pieces of bad news simply compound problems. I repeat, what hurts administrators the most is not what people know but what they do not know. Half a truth, like half a brick, will travel further. I say disclose everything to everybody.

Helpful Hints. Offering tips to others in writing can sound like egotistical nonsense. I hope the following suggestions on communication in a political community will not sound that way, or if they do, that they will be forgiven.

Sometimes it helps to leave a paper trail. In these litigious times when critical issues are discussed, understandings should be written down. A memorandum dictated in front of all parties is an excellent device. Then misunderstandings can be repaired on the spot. The memo should be as brief as possible and strictly factual. It can save a lot of "you said, I said" exchanges later if the record is fairly complete. And the importance of leaving a paper trail in any matter that may later involve lawyers cannot be overemphasized, even though it is a diffcult thing to do and seems a little paranoid. Related to this, but perhaps not quite as heavy, is the practice of finishing conversations by saying, "All right, let's pin it down. Where do we stand? Here is my understanding. Correct me if I'm wrong."

Another useful suggestion, mentioned previously, is to have several levels of administrators in the office at the same time when discussing critical issues and when giving instructions. The successful industry president who offered this advice noted how easily administrative directives can he embezzled away in any organization. This tendency sometimes seems particularly characteristic of the democratic political campus. The president of a corporation attending a campus seminar once cited an example. He came to work one morning and asked a question of a clerk at a window. The clerk, not recognizing him as the president, gave him an incomplete and sarcastic answer. He said nothing to the person but went directly to a meeting with his vice presidents. Still steaming, he reminded them that people form their impressions of an organization on the basis of the first three or four people they meet—usually someone at a window. In something of a controlled bellow, he informed them that he wanted the company to be warm and concerned about people. He stressed the importance of such an atmosphere to a favorable public relations impression. He urged the vice presidents to adopt as a high priority item on their agendas the implementation of this directive. Later, he heard how the fire was embezzled away. One vice president, who was apparently typical in his behavior, went to a meeting of his own staff and began by saying, "Oh, by the way, before we get started, the old man's on a tear because he got a snotty answer from someone at a window downstairs. He wants us to warm the place up. Now, what's the first item of business?" The advantage of having at least two levels of management in to receive critical instructions is that managers at one level will reinforce those at another. The possibility that instructions will be ignored is reduced.

The Symbolic Presidency

In the university regarded as a political community, the presidency is clearly symbolic in times of campus travail. In the words of Daniel Bell (1971, p. 170), "In situations of conflict or stress, the university, like any institution, needs a rallying symbol and this symbol is, necessarily, the president of the institution." It is also apparent, however, that the president is politically symbolic in the day-to-day life of the institution and not just in crisis. The president changes the chemistry of every meeting he or she attends. His symbolic presence is requested for every gathering. And the president is appreciated and rewarded for such attendance. Thus a president who stays on campus is usually more appreciated than an off-campus president; after all, one of the first rules of politics is "Be there." Because of the symbolism of the office, he enters into the fabric of every relationship and is the focus of blame or credit for the endeavors of the institution. He represents the strength of the university's unity of purpose. He is the reducer of ambiguity in an ambiguous world, the symbol of fairness in an imperfect world. The list could go on. The president also becomes a symbol of the style that he espouses. His presence is one of the factors that forces people to accept the assumptions of a style and make it work. There are times when the president must ceremonially wear the crown and other times when he must wear the bell.

It's easy for a president to miss the effect of the symbolism of his or her position. I have heard presidents say in egotistical exasperation, "That so and so dean fooled around with that committee for three months and couldn't get anything out of them. All they needed was a firm hand and a little coaxing. I went before that committee and got everything I wanted inside of two hours." The president should not overestimate his personal genius in such situations; it is the office of the president that has the power to conjure.

Political Impartiality. The president in his or her symbolic role as a political leader is expected to be fair to all constituencies. Probably this expectation is reflected in the general recognition of the fact that the president generally cannot favor the extremes of faculty opinion. The port and starboard factions of an academic community are vital for balance. They provide correctives to the community and to the administration. They play a role in the political dialectic of the campus. Temperamentally, in my observation, the members of both groups tend to be individuals who are much alike. Outside the areas of their professional expertise, where they are frequently exemplary, they tend to be opinionated, doctrinaire, and binary in their judgments. "You are for us or against us" seems to be the formula often applied to administrators. Consequently, an administrator can seldom run a credit balance with either group for very long. It is sometimes well to have a dean of faculty who is viewed as generally tilting a bit in the direction of one group or another. If this is the case, however, it is best to have a person who leans in the opposite direction somewhere close to the president or the dean of the faculty in the chain of command. In the long term, an administrator does the most consistent and profitable business with the great middle group of the faculty.

The starboard group in the faculty will soon fall out of love with a president who is not so totalitarian as to excite the admiration of Ivan the Terrible—totalitarian, that is, with those of contrary persuasion. Yet starboard faculty members hesitate a bit longer than do the portsiders to go to war against the president because of greater feelings of deference for authority.

The demand that the president be impartial suggests some norms of behavior. A president, or for that matter any administrator, should never go to war on another person's anger. It is a mistake to succumb to the indignation of others. Administrators err gravely if they interfere in personal quarrels, except as an impartial referee or as the *pater familias* who simply decrees that the bickering will stop. I have known presidents and deans who, upon receiving the presentations of a trusted colleague or a close office worker, would call in someone and "land" on him, only to discover, to their complete dismay, that the problem was infinitely more complicated than represented, even though every effort had been made by the carrier of the indignation to be fair.

People tend to report problems to an administrator in a bimodal frame of reference, in a good guys and bad guys context. In stating "facts" freighted with indignation, the reporter always embezzles them to some extent. The reporting, consciously or unconsciously, is oversimplified. As someone has said, "Half the fun of remembering is reinterpreting." The most effective administrators therefore refuse to sign on to the irritations of others in the organization. They spend a great deal of time complimenting colleagues and defending them against the criticism of others. They tend to put favorable interpretations on actions that others may hold to be suspect. And they tend to see things from the point of view of the person being complained about. These are attitudes that spread through the organization.

There are necessary and painful lessons, of course, to be learned from going off on a tear with inadequate information. It is better, however, for each person to learn his own lessons. To use a chauvinist phrase, "Never let someone learn to shave on your beard."

The impartiality requirement also suggests that an administrator should not have his or her decision dictated by another. Sometimes decision issues will come to an administrator with an attempt to commit him to another's agenda. For example: such a presentation might be preceded by a dean's approaching a president with the following comment: "This matter has been appealed to you because we have been unable to agree on a decision. It's all right to listen to all sides, but let me warn you, you must decide in the following fashion for the following reasons." The answer should be, "I will not accept any strictures on my discretion. If the matter comes to me, it means that it hasn't been resolved at a lower level. I get a clean shot. I cannot afford to be the prisoner of anyone. If you want to go back and work on the problems some more, fine. Otherwise, I must make my own decision, and you can count on that decision being unreliable from someone's point of view. Maybe it's your turn."

A relatively minor embezzlement of the obligation to be impartial is the tendency of members of a team to promise to deliver someone else's vote. It violates the spirit of a democratic/political style. A president, for example, may say, "You do your part. I'll handle the board." Or a dean may say, "You take care of the department chairmen. I can deliver the president." When one reflects, this type of derogating statement implies an overly compliant president or board or an overly manipulative administrator. Words do count. The way one says things and the rhetoric that is used subtly influences attitudes.

Another difficulty with promising to deliver someone's vote is that it forecloses the possibility of repair by one's colleagues. Part of the style I am talking about is openness and an emphasis on team problem solving. The promise to deliver a vote commits the promiser to a particular course of action, to a Machiavellianism that is counterproductive. Additionally, if for any reason the person making the promise to deliver someone else's vote cannot deliver it, the promiser has a residual feeling of resentment, a feeling of somehow having been "bagged."

Goal Setting. The symbolic political character of the presidency and of the university generally may be illustrated by the demand nearly always levied on a new president that he or she set goals for the institution. The president is the symbolic leader of the community. Establishing objectives is one of the things that leaders do. So he must be the talking chief when the university's activities are explained to the general public. He must be the war chief when the university must fight for resources. And he must be the chief of councils when wise decisions are to be taken. Somehow it seems to me the demand that the president fix goals for the institution, a demand usually leveled in the opening weeks of his tenure, is a way of asking the president to insert a visible presence and to take command of his jurisdictional territory. The perplexities of leadership occasioned by this demand are discussed in a later chapter.

Interpreter of Events. The symbolic character of the presidency is further illustrated by the importance of the president's role as chief interpreter of campus events. Many occurrences on campus are ambiguous. The president plays a vital part in elucidating to the community what is taking place. Here a consistent philosophy of administration and a consistent perspective on the university can be immensely useful. For example, in the style under discussion, the interpretation of dissent as an acceptable element of the political process is very healing. The interpretation and presentation of the need for procedures as a part of fair and representative governance are vital. Likewise, interpreting the character of the dialectic and the political process is of critical concern.

Finally, the interpretive responsibilities of the office make the dominant mood of the president important to morale in the institution. It may seem empathetic to go along with the prevailing despair and to join in grumbling about the imperfect character of existence. It is a default of the symbolic responsibilities of the presidency. It is best for the university if presidents are optimists even if they must be optimists without hope, as a colleague described himself. Pessimism will not sustain us. Anyway, don't most of us feel with Camus, "Lo, in the middle of the winter I found there was in me an invincible spring"?

Other Clues. One obvious illustration of the symbolic nature of the presidency is the way the campus reputation and popularity of the president follow the fortunes of the institution. In good times the president is usually reasonably popular. In bad times the reverse is true.

There are other, more subtle, clues to this symbolic aspect. For one thing, the path to the final selection of a president is usually relatively narrow. Generally speaking, for instance, administrators from the public sector are not chosen to be presidents of colleges and universities in the independent sector. Ivy League schools overwhelmingly pick individuals who have played work-up through the Ivy League system, beginning with graduation from an Ivy League school. The presidents of large prestigious institutions are similarly selected from those who have in some way been in the bloodline of large schools. Such procedures may be partly justified on the grounds of knowing the territory. One has the feeling, however, that the symbolism of the selection is a very real and perhaps overwhelming factor.

Another small clue may be found in the great difficulties college and university administrators experience in finding a suitable confidant on whom to test ideas and to work through administrative uncertainties. No matter how warm and admiring and objective the individual may be, if the confidant is in any way related to the president's college or university, problems soon surface. The confidant becomes uncomfortable with the role. The president is supposed to be a strong, flawless leader on whom all depend. The revelation of vulnerability is threatening. This "isolation" characteristic is, of course, to be noted in all leadership positions in the society. It is related to the earlier discussion on our need to make heroes of those on whom we depend. The symbolic role of the college and university president, however, makes the problem particularly acute for campus leaders.

Yet another hint of the symbolic character of the presidency is seen in the fact that the way the academic community perceives the president's liberal or conservative leanings influences his or her ability to initiate new programs. A. Lawrence Lowell (1938, p. 21) puts the matter succinctly: "if he desires to innovate he will be greatly helped by having the reputation of being conservative, because the radicals who want a change are little offended by the fact of change, while the conservatives will be likely to follow him because they look on him as sharing their temperament and point of view."

The Vulnerable Presidency

The great carved heads of Easter Island have puzzled archeologists for decades. They stand with their backs to the sea and overlook the land, brooding silently. Through the centuries, many have been mutilated. In some instances, the giant stone heads have been severed from the shoulders, obviously with great effort. Was there some invading band of alien people who desecrated the gods of peaceful islanders? The archeologists once thought so. Now it is their best thinking that after a period of hardship and travail, the people of Easter Island destroyed their own gods, punishing them for the misfortunes that had befallen the people. There is a deep parable here for university leaders. If the silent, unmoving, and, to use the term of current fashion, "uninvolved" gods of Easter Island could be the object of so much hostility, how do you think that in times of continued campus difficulty the symbolic, vulnerable university president will fare?

"Bagged" Any Time. I noted earlier that in the university community, individual leaders are regarded as ancillary and expendable and are therefore also vulnerable. The president is even more open to attack than other campus leaders because he or she has no built-in and stable constituency. Though he may look upon himself as serving the interests of the faculty, staff, and students, these groups frequently do not see his activities in these terms. So the president must construct a constituency as he goes along. The composition of that constituency will shift in membership and size, and the possibility that it may be withdrawn at any time is one of the hazards which he, like any political figure, must face. I do not mean to say that because a president has opposition, and people are unhappy with him, he is always in political difficulty. Of course, there is no president so popular that the day he has a bad cold some people will not take hope that it may go into pneumonia and be fatal. Usually, however, a president is not in major difficulty unless a coalition of discontented constituencies develops. Here again the

political character of the position is evident. The president can weather seasons of faculty unhappiness. But when students and faculty members make common cause, the president would do well to drop other concerns and pay attention.

Apart from this general problem, there are broader, less personal, circumstances that can jeopardize the position of a president. Someone once remarked that deans are appointed for two years and stay for life; presidents are appointed for life and remain in office for two years. The observation overstates the situation, but it is true that a president can be in difficulties on short notice. A case in point: A group of students waited on a newly appointed president to announce their satisfaction in the selection of an individual with whom they could work. They congratulated the new president on his reputation for understanding students and for generally enlightened points of view. Then, almost casually, they announced their intention of showing on the campus one of the more widely publicized X-rated movies in the next few days. The reason for the showing was that the local porn house had refused to exhibit the film on the ground that the publicity would call down too much heat. The decision reflected the prudence of the theater owner, not moral sensitivity, since films of comparable candor, but of less renown, were consistently shown. The students felt that the attitude of the theater owner was unreasonable; ergo, they had decided to present the film on campus. At this point, the president said, "Sit down, scholars. Let me show you how easily you can bag a president. All you have to do is to show this film according to plan. If I forbid the showing, then understandably you will be annoyed and so will large numbers of the faculty and a few influential people in the community. You will charge me with being a bluenose who knows what pornography is when the Supreme Court cannot decide with workable precision. The university is supposed to be a free market for ideas. The charge will be 'the president is playing censor and moral czar for the campus and the community.' If, on the other hand, I permit the film to be shown, the community at large, and some campus people, will charge that the academic community has enthusiastically accepted the president because he is a permissive idiot, running a cesspool of sheltered and privileged sin, and that neither he nor the institution is worthy of support." The president pointed out that this was only the opening episode in the scenario and that, repeated eight or nine times, such an episode could mean the end of a presidential career. In this particular case, the students decided not to show the controversial film. The decision could have been different.

There are other circumstances that can bag a president. In a fierce economy move, the governor of the state announces that the public colleges and universities must operate, in the next year, on budgets 10 percent below those in force. The legislature concurs. After valiant efforts by campus administrators have failed to reverse the decision, and after extensive and unhappy consultation with appropriate campus groups, the university strains mightily to adjust to the cuts. Equipment and supply accounts are stripped. Telephones are removed from offices. Travel funds are eliminated. Repairs to buildings are postponed. Not enough! With great agony and with understandable hubbub among the faculty, staff members and students, part-time instructors are notified that they will not be reemployed the following year. A few senior professors close to retirement, and some not so close but with independent means, are called in for lengthy conversations by the dean and the president. There are some "voluntary" early retirements. The job of cutting the budget has been done for the first year. It is, of course, a bad year. Tempers are short. Minor incidents become the source of major irritations. Tendencies to cannibalism appear in departments. Accusations of unfair treatment surface everywhere. Charges of fiscal privilege are leveled against the administration and against other departments and even colleagues in the same department.

The drama is not finished. The next year the governor and legislature announce with considerable and perhaps justifiable satisfaction that a few small necessary increases have been granted in a few critical areas of higher education. Beyond these increases, however, public colleges and universities will operate on a "hold fast" budget for the next year. No further cuts will be necessary, but, regrettably, the mandated salary increases for state employees, including members of academic communities, will have to come out of present operating budgets. Pandemonium. The outcry from the campuses is matched by retributive legislative proposals to investigate teaching loads, administrative efficiency, and admission requirements. The universities are more sorely pressed than most state agencies, some of which have the flexibility to cut budgets by temporary layoffs and by "releasing" employees in the middle of the year. The pressure mounts. After many heavy discussions and adrenalized meetings, it is obvious that personnel cuts for the campus are inevitable, and the events of the succeeding weeks offer a preliminary glimpse of the apocalypse. The year is one of unbelievable turmoil and unhappiness. Naturally, the president does not escape his share of hostility as the most visible symbol of the university and now the symbol of its hardship. He is accused of an astonishing and imaginative array of malfeasances, nonfeasances, and misfeasances. He nevertheless survives the spring. In the meantime, he has risen to magnificent heights of imagination and energy in fund raising, peacemaking, lobbying, and public relations.

Still, denouement is yet to come. The budget cycle begins again. Word comes down from the capital that the only decision that will be seriously considered by the legislature and the governor is whether to cut the operating budgets of the universities by 5 percent or 10 percent. The rest is predictable, the only uncertainty being whether the president will resign voluntarily or be asked to leave by the trustees, faculty, and the students, in a chorus. It is permissible, of course, to add or subtract a year or two from this time schedule.

In spite of the seeming relationship of specific incidents to presidential exit from office, generally speaking, the process seems to be almost impersonal. The political and symbolic character and operation of a university campus are nowhere better illustrated than in the fact that when a president is under pressure to leave, a kind of consensus that it is time for the president to depart somehow develops at almost every level of the institution. Sometimes that consensus seems to have been reached almost unwillingly but there is a general recognition that a change is necessary. "Presidential performance may have remained unchanged or even improved by any set of reasonable standards. Suddenly criticisms of the president formerly shrugged off by most faculty and students are taken seriously. Since as a culture we demand reasons, reasons for discontent appear. Careful observation leaves the impression that they are really peripheral. The decision that a change is needed seems basically impersonal and unrelated to presidential performance. The agenda has simply changed" (Walker, 1977c, p. 57).

I believe the exit of a president, in a large number of cases, can be understood by examining the leadership behavior of animals in packs. I recall, though not in detail, an article about wolves that offered a couple of eyebrow-raising theories in describing the death of the old leader and the selection of a new wolf to head the pack. Contrary to popular stereotype, the leader was not killed by the strongest male with the most testosterone the minute his back legs became shaky. It was obvious for some time that five or six of the larger and younger males in the pack could kill the leader at any time. The pack simply would not let the leader be challenged until there was kind of a group consensus that the time was right for a change in leadership. When that consensus occurred, one of the large males, but not always the largest, was permitted to challenge. When the leader went down, several other males joined in what seemed to be almost a mercy killing. I recall also that the pack had gone through a kind of unconscious selection process in picking the male who would be the next leader. One of the characteristics for which he was apparently chosen was concern for the young. When trouble threatened, the wolf who was to be permitted to challenge the leader would run and stand over the cubs. I doubt that he was running for office. The pack sensed that in this characteristic there was survival value.

I think this scenario, zoologically accurate or not, presents an appropriate analogy. When the time is right, all kinds of reasons surface for being critical of the president.* The fact that all kinds of seemingly trumped up criticisms will surface probably accounts for such cynical presidential statements as, "You never know who your enemies are until you are down."

---

*Parenthetically, I should mention that one of the topics that comes up fairly frequently in such discussions is presidential houses. So frequently, in fact, that a word of survival advice to new presidents would include, "Don't let them build you a new house. The building of a new, expensive residence will ultimately be defined as a crime, or at least a sin, for which your successor will be forgiven."

Enemies Revealed. I have heard a number of unfrocked administrators, particularly presidents, complain with bitterness, "When the lion begins to weaken, the jackals gather." Or, "I never knew how many enemies I had until I got into difficulty. Then I was astonished at the number of people that I considered to be friends who turned on me." One of the mistakes that administrators make is to fail to recognize the extent to which praise, appreciation, and support come to them not because of their special qualities as human beings but because of the office they occupy. It is the office to which people pay deference and burn the incense. Similarly, when an administrator comes under attack, it is really the office more than the person that is under fire, even though the exercise may seem highly personal.

In the long patience of time, the process is one that usually is healthy for the university. Having different people move in and out of the leadership spots is undoubtedly good for a democratic institution. The vulnerability of presidents and the rather impersonal nature of the circumstances that account for their exits are truly among the more graphic illustrations of the fact that the university does indeed operate like a political/democratic community.

A governor of an eastern state when he lost an election declared, "I was defeated by the rise in the price of hamburger." He was probably right. The implication for administrators is that presidents should not be lulled into the feeling that they will have a tremendous amount of loyal, active, and ready support in difficult times. When trouble comes, even though the cause is just, the support for a president will not be as enthusiastic as he or she might feel is deserved and justified by the splendor of the cause. An illustration: an influential political figure calls the president to say in effect, but less bluntly, "I have two outstanding people that I want appointed to positions in your institution. If these appointments do not go through and immediately, you will receive a 10 percent cut in your operating budget for next year." The president is in a box. The legislator may be bluffing or overestimating his own power to influence the budget process, although it is reasonable to assume that he may have such power. If the president capitulates, there will be difficulties. Apart from the ethical question involved, the quality of the candidates proposed is not incontestably high. University procedures call for a search and screen for most positions. Furthermore, affirmative-action requirements do not permit appointments on a political basis. The president's reputation for a stiff backbone will be badly damaged if he capitulates or is suspected of capitulating to the pressure of the legislator. Additionally, the issue is not one simply of personal morality and courage. The welfare of the institution may be on the line in the president's decision. The president begins to make inquiries to see how much support he will have if he finds himself in open warfare with the legislative leadership. He's surprised and shocked to find that people are very guarded in their willingness to agree that he is unequivocally right and very hesitant to embrace a potential political leper. Whatever the president decides, he should be willing to pay the price and recognize that political behavior is characteristic of the university and appropriate to its character as a pluralistic democracy. Whatever happens as a result of the president's decision may not be all bad, just as it will not be all good.

Self-Defense. Because attacks on the president should not be regarded as in their genetic structure personal does not mean that administrators do not have a right to defend themselves. Administrators are entitled to the same sense of injustice and the same privileges of self-defense as any other citizen. They lose their citizenship if and when they go to the state penitentiary, not when they assume the office of the president. I think a cartoon I once saw is appropriate. Two proper British explorers in pith helmets are up to their necks in quicksand and one is saying, "Quicksand or not, I have a half a mind to struggle." Why not? But keep in mind the symbolic character of the presidency. It is important when deciding such critical questions as whether to be present or absent when trouble starts and the president's stewardship is being examined. The symbolic character of the presidency would indicate that the presence of the president will change the tone of the meeting. The general rule is, "Be there." Many a president who has chosen to take a much overdue vacation just when things are the hottest on the rationalization, "let 'em make up their own minds; I'll stand on my record," is asking for it. Criticisms are much more measured and the standards of evidence higher when the president is there. Given the decision to struggle, the question becomes,

What are the best tactics? Does a soft answer turn away wrath?
When under attack, is nothing the wisest thing to say and do? Does
vigorous counterattack provide the best opportunity for effectively
deflecting the spears? I suspect, having watched dozens of cases
over the years, that it doesn't make much difference. When they're
after ya, they're after ya. Do what is most comfortable. The evidence simply isn't in on the effectiveness of the various strategies
available. Effectiveness may be highly idiosyncratic, depending on
a host of variables. Some presidents arrange to "throw a baby out
of the sleigh" when the wolves get too close. I've known two or
three who did rather well by pushing a dean forward as an expendable sacrifice when the howling got too loud. Sometimes a
president is saved by being able to identify and direct attention
toward an outside enemy: the legislature, the governor, or a local
newspaper unreasonable enough to draw the fire. Freud was right.
An organization can gain real morale benefits from having an outside enemy.

I believe it was Mayor Daley who once advised that the secret
of political survival was "Don't back no losers. Don't make no
waves." It is advice that most presidents would disdain to accept,
and even if they did accept such a strategy, it might not work in
a university presidency. The symbolic requirements and ideological commitments of the job make it in some ways politically more
demanding than being the mayor of a city. I think in the final analysis the best thing an administrator can do to maintain his own
psychological equilibrium is to arrange in advance for a retreat
position and to join the KMA Club (K standing for "kiss"). Do what
feels right.

Holy War

Holy war is the process whereby complex issues of the head
are translated into simple issues of the heart for large numbers of
people. The campus disorders and demonstrations of the '60s first
highlighted and focused attention on the phenomenon. Such pro-
tests and demonstrations continue to occur on many campuses.
They are not now as well publicized and no longer defined in
strongly pathological terms. Such events, in my view, cannot be

simply dismissed as some incomprehensible aberration of the troubled '60s. The phenomenon of holy war provides valuable clues to the way universities function and must be incorporated into coherent views of campuses and administrative styles. Everyone, including academics, had been aware for years or decades that campuses were capable of explosive reactions. But the disruptions and upsets of earlier times had about them the tonality of panty raids or spring madness, gone slightly awry. They seemed more related to the exuberant and unrestrained vitality of aggregated youth than to pathology. The '60s were different. There was a consistency, a pattern, an ugliness about the major campus disorders that prompted people to explore seriously the pathological model. One of the more careful analyses of this kind has been done by Rufus Miles (1969), whose work is profound and deserves careful attention. I would suggest, however, that the pathology model may not be as useful as more functional political explanations of campus rebellions. The problem is not that campuses somehow broke down, became disorganized, and failed to function properly, but rather that they became organized in such a way that they produced "holy war."

The meaning of such events for administration bears some thought befringed with wonder. Many of the campus disruptions of the '60s had about them a kind of an inexorability, a sort of impersonality and consistency that makes them seem, even in retrospect, to be something alien, imposed on the campus and not a part of it. To a degree, this is true. Universities did not react to these disruptions in their usual style of meeting difficulties. There were reasons for this. Campuses found their options severely restricted. They were almost forced to respond in ways that made the holy-war drama unfold according to the scenario planned and executed by organized dissident students. In one sense, campus disorders were produced by off-campus forces. The enormity of the pressures brought to bear on university administrators when such disruptions took place is almost impossible to comprehend. There was tremendous public pressure for "law and order." And because of pronouncements of political figures at the national level, major campus disruptions were defined in the public mind as criminal behavior. All of the hostility and anxiety occasioned by the "crime wave," real or imagined, perceived as sweeping through the society, fastened on student demonstrations as a visible confirmation of the fear that criminals were taking over the nation as the morale and fiber of the society broke down.

Another influence that made sit-ins and demonstrations difficult for campus administrators to manage was the attention lavished upon the phenomena by the mass media, particularly by television stations. It was television in particular that built the crowds of people that gathered outside administration buildings. Crowd pressure was the necessary prerequisite for demonstrators to succeed in achieving their demands. Had public attention not focused so dramatically and emotionally on demonstrations, the problems could have been handled much more adequately and antiseptically.

Still, even these pressures might have been manageable had there not been such enormous public demand—by politicians, by indignant taxpayers, and by concerned citizens generally—for immediate solutions. Campus administrators had no time margin in which to work things out. The problem-solving system in the university, which had operated in a milieu of negotiation, conciliation, and adjustment, had worked well on the whole. Faculty members and administrators had, in most instances, been quite responsive to students, in spite of the stereotype presented by campus disrupters of cold and impersonal treatment. Although it is true that most campuses were and are too indifferent to the daily bureaucratic irritations experienced by students, the concerns of the '60s were even deeper. And in such a charged situation, the demand for instant solutions, for instant retaliation, for premature calling in of the police or of the National Guard complicated matters immeasurably. It created an atmosphere in which holy war could develop.

Even allowing for the dependence of holy war on off-campus pressures, if the phenomenon is seen as an extreme political expression, rather than the breakdown of social organization, it becomes more comprehensible. Such a conflict, after all, was in microcosm an intense and well-publicized manifestation of movements in the larger society. Let us look at the final campus outcome of many demonstrations. First, holy war reemphasized the need for institutions to be oriented to their constituencies, a political fact of life. A friend once told me of an incident that occurred in the office of the chancellor of a large and prestigious Western university. The chancellor was talking with a group of angry minority students. They had presented him with a set of what were, for the most part, reasonable "demands." They were, however, demands that overlapped a number of jurisdictions in the university. The chancellor spent considerable time explaining the steps that would be necessary before changes in procedures could be made. One of the protesting students interrupted the chancellor to inquire mildly, "Would it speed things up, Chancellor, if we set fire to the drapes?" The chancellor is said to have later ruefully remarked to a colleague, "The sad thing is that setting fire to the drapes *would* have speeded things up."

Some curriculum changes resulted from holy war. More than this, there was a loosening of the process of curricular change on some campuses. It is true, of course, that the institutions paid a political price for public convulsions. The dialectic called forth right-wing repressive reactions, strengthened the authoritarian impulses of some central systems, spawned hosts of campus regulations by off-campus agencies, and damaged the credibility of faculty members and administrators in proportion to the alarm and indignation of constituents.

There was also a more subtle legacy. Student leaders often discovered that indignation is no substitute for planning, that disruption provides no agenda for the future, that high moral vision is inadequate justification for totalitarianism. Many student leaders seem to have recognized that campus channels can be made to work more effectively than they do, if effort is applied with patience, determination, and intelligence. In sum, the end results of the holy wars were political in character.

Their effects on some colleges and universities were the kinds of effects sometimes pursued and achieved in political arenas by other political means. The political character of the tactics used strengthens the impression that the process was an extreme manifestation of a political impulse and strategy. Like political change elsewhere in society, the campus disorders probably arose from a general feeling of imperfections in the world. As we well know, an unpopular, unholy war was in progress at the time. Campuses were not happy places. Similar kinds of discontent and unhappiness were, of course, disseminated widely throughout the society. Academics, however, perhaps more than others, entertain visions of Camelot, and properly so. Universities, it sometimes seems, do not compare themselves with Harvard. They compare themselves with Heaven. By this exalted standard they fall short. The result is a free-floating discontent that is stronger than that in most democratic organizations. Academics do not suffer fools gladly and do not always accept hardship as a normal part of the human circumstance. Out of this discontent, good things as well as bad things can develop. In the '60s, however, this ambience provided ammunition for the explosions.

In Miles' analysis of these phenomena as pathological breakdown, he compares campus disruptions with disorders in the War Relocation Authority Camp at Posten, Arizona, noting similarities in the stages of the "breakdown." First of all, trust declines. Then follow (1) the stage of the festering sore, a long period during which people are disenchanted with "the administration"; (2) the beginning of organized defiance; (3) the period of indecision by the administration; (4) the crackdown; (5) the smoldering aftermath; and (6) the rebuilding stage (1969, pp. 356-359).

I do not set aside Miles' analysis, even though it uses a pathology model. His description of the stages of "pathological breakdown" is a good account of what happens on a campus when holy war develops. However, the development of the scenario need not be seen as entirely pathological. Look at some of the results.

From the point of view of political effect, such disruptions many times focused effective popular concern. As previously indicated, that transformation is often a necessary part of the politicizing process. The disorders also served to challenge leadership and sometimes to transfer it. Often this process took the form of forcing administrators out of nonpartisan, mediating, and judicial roles where they could present themselves as presiding over fair procedures. The demonstrators viewed the neutral role as corrupt, considering the appeal to impartial and fair procedures and to due process as the refuge of pimps for the status quo. The phenomenon John Chancellor referred to as the "extreme center" developed. Thus the impartial position became the focus of all radical action. The demonstrators' next step was to make corrupt any other position than their own. Anything other than an orthodox and violently partisan position became unacceptable. This step was approached gradually. At first, as rallies continued to escalate the action, administrators were told that their neutrality would be respected. They were simply asked to be present at the rally to answer questions and to state their impartiality. But they were then made to appear thoroughly uninformed or insensitive on moral issues. The radicals asked them very specific and detailed factual questions, usually about Vietnam. If they said they did not know the answers, they were booed. Answers that seemed too intellectual or too footnotey were hooted down. If the administrator suggested that no one had authoritative answers to certain questions, he was also booed. The person appearing before the crowd was made to look like the hireling of a totalitarian regime. The formula then became, "We can do nothing about the tyranny overseas. That's thousands of miles away. We don't have to. The tyranny overseas is here in residence at our university. An attack on the administration of the university is a blow for truth and justice everywhere in the world. All tyrannies will be resolved in this arena of combat."

In the meantime as the drama unfolded, the protesting groups indulged in pushing, provoking, and challenging behavior, occasionally sallying over the line into violence, but never quite far enough to be obvious to most of the academic community. The strategy was to provoke the administration into some sort of action that could be represented to the campus as peremptory, high-handed, and totalitarian. The off-campus pressures increased rapidly. Sooner or later most administrators acted out their roles in the disrupters' play. The rapidity with which wavering campus opinion then solidified behind the protesters angered and bewildered university authorities. For the full drama to be enacted with the "trashing" of buildings and other pathologies, the issues had to be perceived by campus constituencies as light against darkness, truth against lies, compromise against conscience, peace against war.

Of course, there were elements, strong elements, of pathology in evidence. I do not mean to gloss over the terrible human costs paid by individuals and campuses when such scenes unfolded.

I would only argue that the model with the most promise of avoiding such scenarios in the long future is political. The model of the decline of the West, the decline of morality, the crime wave, or even institutional decay really leads to no realistic strategies for solution. The political view of campus disorders reemphasizes the usefulness of negotiating skills for administrators, the importance of trust, and the need to maintain the allegiance of the middle opinion group to avoid or mitigate political mass movements such as those involved in holy war.

Finally, the threat of political convulsion on troubled campuses should focus attention administratively on the perpetual need to deal with low-grade infections that keep elevated the temperature of the campus.

Four

Exerting Leadership in an Active-Reactive Environment

The central hypothesis of this book, as I'm sure is clear by now, is that a university operates like a political community, undergirded by the ideology of a pluralistic democracy. The behavior of a campus, however, goes beyond the theorems and charts of political science.

The Organismic Process Orientation

There are processes in the university that the star administrators of my acquaintance have detected and used intuitively or in full awareness. In general, these can be subsumed under some such aphorism as "the university has a life of its own." The problem is how to clarify this awareness for the practicing administrator so that it can be used and built into an administrative style. I have

85

chosen a concept taken from biology—that of homeostasis. This concept, as originally used by Walter B. Cannon, refers to plants and animals being composed of interrelated, interdependent, and self-balancing systems. I will attempt to draw no tortured parallels between such organisms and the university. Some set of spectacles, however, is necessary. I do not present this comparison for the sake of theoretical pushups; nor do I intend to establish another model. I am simply trying to highlight phenomena of administrative life that are too often ignored because we have no way to see them as a whole. Lacking a positive perspective, we retreat to the pathological model and deal in our styles with processes that are natural in the university as though, indeed, they were diseased. Once again, the latent pathological model of university events asserts itself. The concept of homeostasis, as I shall use it here, is designed to place the following phenomena in the context of the natural physiology of the university:

1. The university is an active, bubbling place, not an inert mass. It is not simply standing and waiting to be moved by administrative effort. It is moving all the time and vigorously.
2. The university operates as a unity—not every day and everyway—but it is far less particularistic and divided as a reacting entity than the organization charts would suggest. Someone once remarked that a university is like a snake: If you poke it in one place, it wiggles all over.
3. Universities have strong self-correcting tendencies. When bacteria invade the tissue of an organism, counterreactions are immediately called forth, because the systems of that organism exist in a moving equilibrium. And therefore interference in one system calls forth compensating reactions in other systems. So with the university.
4. Closely related to the counterreactive properties of organisms is the tendency to resist change, a tendency that is both natural and healthy. So it is in universities.

Although the view of the university as a homeostatic organization has not been deeply explored, the operation of seemingly homeostatic processes has been remarked in similar organizations.

The comments of a sympathetic scientist about the Marine Biological Laboratory in Woods Hole are illustrative:

> The Marine Biological Laboratory in Woods Hole is a paradigm, a human institution possessed of a life of its own, self-regenerating, touched all around by human meddle but constantly improved, embellished by it. The place was put together, given life, sustained in today's version of its maturity and prepared for further elaboration and changes in its complexity, by what can only be described as a bunch of people. Neither the spectacularly eminent men who have served as directors down through the century nor the numberless committees by which it is seasonally raddled nor even the trustees, have ever been able to do more than hold the lightest reins over this institution; it seems to have a mind of its own, which it makes up in its own way . . . . It is amazing that such an institution, exerting so much influence on academic science, has been able to remain so absolutely autonomous. It has, to be sure, linkages of various kinds, arrangements with outside universities for certain graduate programs, and it adheres delicately, somewhat ambiguously, to the Woods Hole Oceanographic Institute just up the street. But it has never come under the domination of any outside institution or governmental agency, nor has it ever been told what to do by any outside group. *Internally, the important institutional decisions seem to have been made by a process of accommodation and adaptation, with resistable forces always meeting movable objects* [Emphasis added; Thomas, 1974, pp. 58–60].

One reason the homeostatic view has not been applied vigorously and systematically to the university is the preemptive dominance of the pathological view of puzzling behavior on university campuses. I can hear the objections to this statement: "Do you mean to tell me all the maneuvering, howling, jockeying for position, intemperate memoranda, goof-off committees, and puerile academic senate sessions can possibly mean anything other than slightly restrained, self-serving pandemonium?" Or again, "Isn't it obvious that Robert Hutchins was right in his view that whatever their protestations to the contrary, faculty members really prefer anarchy to any form of government?" Such objections come from administrators who see "problem" behavior as the breakdown of organization rather than as organizational principles at work. An effective working model of administration requires a more positive attitude toward the seemingly perverse or random activities that occur on a campus. So it would seem worthwhile to examine some of the behavioral and administrative characteristics of the university through homeostatic lenses.

An Active Organism

The fact that a university has a mind of its own is usually noted by some beleaguered administrator unhappy about the realization that his lofty and obviously better-informed, more objective, and more commendable views are being resisted by the organization. A prominent and articulate university president seems to be saying something of this sort in a much-quoted article: "I had become the victim of a vast, amorphous, unwitting, unconscious conspiracy to prevent me from doing anything whatever to change the university's status quo"(Bennis, 1973, p. 17). It is strange that few administrators, supposedly rational and analytical human beings, trained in the arts of dispassionate analysis, have not been more suspicious of the ways in which universities resist administrative direction. There is a deeper meaning here than appears in the initial reactions to frustration.

Other facts also should have raised questions about that "mind of its own" characteristic. Universities have functioned with some frequency for several months with no president at all, sometimes with only a loosely coordinated committee to direct things. Strong presidents have died while the university, supposedly held together only by the heart-strangling pace of the chief administrator, proceeded with disturbing serenity. The nature of that persistent quality of operation in universities deserves more careful attention, as does the way in which the organization seems to transact its day-to-day business in a kind of moving exchange of adjustments.

Another, perhaps more dramatic, illustration of the university's active will is the way an academic community will deviate from the announced program of the president, or will detour from the master plan, to develop programs that have not been announced or planned in a systematic fashion. I've talked with a number of presidents over the years who have mentioned with pride some program or another for which they assumed parental responsibility. But discussing the program with the people who ran it day-to-day, I have sometimes found that the president actually opposed it to begin with. Only after everyone else realized the program was in place to stay did the president sign on. For instance, a department asks a president when it will be permitted to offer a major. (Most experienced presidents have received such requests.) The president is expected to pledge his or her full and unrelenting support for the development of such a major. Instead, he reluctantly informs the department that there is no place for a major in colloquial Amharic at the university. The president is content with the present services and majors being offered in languages; he may also express uneasiness that enrollment in language courses is on the decline. But the department does not take no for an answer. It begins vigorously recruiting among language students, drums up support from influential and wealthy patrons in the community, offers institutes on weekends and during the summer. Typewriters are heard behind departmental office doors late on Friday afternoons. Department meetings are even called on Saturday mornings. To everyone's amazement, a major emerges that is vigorous and sound. Almost before the president is aware, the department has "crawled up" on him. Not only is there a major, but the major is attracting regional or even nationwide attention.

On a few occasions I have seen the opposite phenomenon. A president blesses some discipline as a logical focus of institutional emphasis and effort. Often, of course, if there are dollars available to be taken "off the top," his or her recommendations are followed. Sometimes, however, the fire and vigor that first called the department to the attention of the president and the university community seems to be diminished by the president's decree that a "pinnacle of excellence" will exist in this area. On rare occasions, a kind of pathology seems to develop. The top professors stop working overtime, lean back against the wall, and wait for the money truck to back up and unload. Such events are not common, but they do occur and they do need to be considered if we are to understand the way university communities behave.

If such reactions are seen as predictable and healthy, a strategy other than executive decree suggests itself. This is for the president or board of trustees to lay out the rules by which departments and academic areas can compete for "pinnacle"status. Even in lean budget years, incentive money can be set aside to reward such competitive efforts. Certainly such rules could not include the requirement that faculty members work overtime. In my observation, however, faculty members do not have to be encouraged to put in extra time when projects are exciting. Most faculty members put in longer hours than are suspected by the general public and often by administrators, in any case. If this incentive strategy seems a little anarchical, I would simply point out that many presidents and boards embrace it unaware, without creating overwhelming disasters. The sort of conversation that now sets such a strategy in motion might begin, "Dr. Vigor, I do understand your desire to get this important program under way. We agree with your view that the program is indeed a significant one and would be useful, if not essential, to many of our students. Regretfully, funds are very limited, as you know. We have decided to allocate the discretionary funds available to us in areas where they will serve as 'multipliers'; in other words, where money can be used to attract grants or gifts from outside the institution. We are committed to supplying 'seed money.' I know that outside resources are difficult to attract, but we've found that such resources are available when programs are important to a university and its constituents. The reserve we have will not be allocated for another two or three months. At that time, I am afraid we will give most favorable consideration to those programs that have been able to attract the promise of such supplemental support from outside. You might see what you can do and then get back to us."

Unified Reactions

Campus demonstrations in the '60s made it apparent to everyone that campuses are capable of unified, if violent, reaction. But universities operate as a unit in more subtle ways too. They seem to have moods that affect the whole entity, for example. When a certain atmosphere exists, touchy issues can be pushed vigorously with satisfactory results. At other times solutions to problems must be finessed. Indeed, one of the key sensitivities of an effective administrator is an awareness of the proper time to push. Sometimes pushing for closure can simply set people up in cement. On other occasions, the failure to push can mean that precious opportunities for movement and problem solving have been sacrificed.

The awareness that a campus on many occasions reacts as a unitary organism is an important one for administrators. Good executives develop an attitude, a feel, and a style that fit this organismic kind of world—a way of perceiving problems, and a way of approaching them. They develop an intuition for how a campus will react and they trust that insight.

Self-Corrective Mechanisms

Effective administrators also sense the reactive and self-corrective qualities of campuses and incorporate this awareness in their styles. Although I have expressed these characteristics in biological terms, others have used metaphors from the physical sciences. One university president of long experience comments, for example: "any collegiate community, particularly in its faculty members and students, is essentially a self-correcting apparatus. It has its own gyros that will ultimately keep it stabilized and afloat" (Healy, 1978, p. 6). I have also heard Newton's third law of motion paraphrased by a number of seasoned administrators over the years. "For every administrative action there is an equal and opposite reaction." But whether perceived through the homeostatic lens or through physical science models, the phenomenon being described is indeed a real one.

Often, as I noted earlier, the reaction is portrayed as though it were diseased. I believe one reason for this portrayal is that the reactive character of campuses is most apparent as a kind of pain response. Many administrators have been thunderstruck by the aggressive and intemperate reactions of faculty members when, in answer to faculty cries for "leadership," a plan to reorganize the university has been developed and presented to the academic community. And central offices of multicampus systems are shocked at the pandemonium released when, having studied matters for months, they announce the assignment of a special emphasis and mission for each institution in the system. These administrators would be less surprised if they recognized that any plan to disrupt the status quo, however rational and well-prepared it may be, will be experienced by some as an attack on the organism that creates pain and defensive reactions.

The Pulse-Pendulum Reaction. In a less dramatic form, the action-reaction qualities of university behavior have been compared with the diastolic and systolic operation of the heart as well as with a pendulum. A dramatic example of the pulse-pendulum on a campus may be observed in the selection of presidents. I have noticed the surprising regularity with which a new president appears to be chosen as an antidote to his predecessor. If the president being replaced is a fiscal type, a facts-and-figures man relatively cold in personal relationships, the next president will have a personality you can warm your hands on. He will relate well to others and have few business skills. "Oh, he'll know something about budgets," as a distinguished colleague has remarked. "He'll know that the debit column is toward the window." I have also observed that when a university has been through two or three presidents in a relatively short time, the "pendulum" tends to stop in the middle. An inside person is often chosen. He or she will have a low profile and a reputation for fairness and hard work.

A similar balancing tendency can be seen in the selection of deans. If a dean has been regarded as generally liberal, his successor will be regarded as generally more conservative, and about as far from the middle line as his predecessor was in the other direction.

Consequently, new presidents and deans are usually treated, in the early weeks of their appointment, to a barrage of presentations in which they are congratulated for not conducting themselves like their predecessors. They are told repeatedly that they have been picked because they have different qualities from the person they are succeeding. Joseph Kaufman (1977) has found that presidents "often . . . identified their roles or challenges as counteracting a predecessor." One of the presidents Kaufman quotes commented: "My predecessor had very bad relations with the faculty, and I was brought here to overcome this." Another president stated: "My predecessor did not face up to the serious financial problems (or retrenchment need) and I was told that this would be my top priority." It is surprising how many presidents and deans fail to detect a pattern in this phenomenon. I have met very few presidents who, at some point in a conversation, were not willing to offer the information that one of their principal accomplishments was to have repaired the damages done to their institutions under previous administrations. Or, if the matter is not addressed so bluntly, it is sometimes suggested in such statements as "It has taken me three years to get things back together again."

There are other illustrations of the operation of the pulse-pendulum principle, perhaps trivial but revealing. I have noticed that when some administrator is singled out for recognition and the bestowal of honors, a "morning after" feeling often creeps over the campus. "What did we do?" "What did we say?" During the following weeks, even though such comments may not come to the attention of the celebrated individual, considerable criticism and complaint can be heard about his or her performance and stewardship.

The political dialectic of a campus, discussed earlier, is another instance of the operation of the pulse-pendulum principle. The principle, however, is more generalized than this dialectic process, as we see in the following example from a different setting. After rioting students destroyed a branch of the Bank of America near the University of California's Santa Barbara campus, Louis Lundborg (1970), chairman of the board of the bank, observed, "I am not afraid the left-wing radicals will win. I'm only afraid of how they will be defeated. The natural sequel to left-wing radical rebellion is right-wing reaction and repression."

Still other examples from the broader society concern the activities of the Food and Drug Administration and the automotive industry. It appears that after the FDA goes through a period of approving many new drugs, problems, complaints, and abuses develop. Then comes the reaction and a period of retrenchment, during which it is difficult to get any new drug approved. Similarly, the automobile companies, which for many years seemed concerned primarily with style, are now experiencing a reactive ad-

justment, characterized by a demand for a strong emphasis on pas-
senger safety.

All these illustrations show, I think, the basic need of organisms, from simple creatures to complex human organizations,
to achieve a state of balance or homeostasis. The swings from one
side to the other, the actions and reactions, can therefore be interpreted as a natural part of the entity's self-correcting mechanisms.

Adjusting to Individual Administrators. A somewhat different
sort of example of the reactive character of universities may be
found in the way academic communities adjust to the characteristics of individual administrators. Those actions an administrative
officer can be counted on to perform will enter into the equation
of the decision-making process. Thus, for example, if a dean of
the faculty accepts as one of his role responsibilities the vetoing of
academic appointments that do not entirely fit the needs of the
department, the certainty of the veto will be programmed into departmental decisions. Since the department will feel sure that the
names will not survive, it will be much more willing to send forward
frivolous recommendations for reasons of friendship or politics.
The department chairman can always say with a shrug, "Well, at
least I tried. You know how the dean is." Or, in a slightly less political context, the department will simply be more casual about
checking out the strengths and weaknesses of candidates.

A kind of mirror-image reinforcement of the view that campuses adjust to the behavior of administrators is demonstrated
when executives moving from one institution to another find
themselves faced with the same problems. The president who has
difficulty with insubordinate deans at one institution will find the
same difficulty at his next institution. The president who has difficulties with a "crown prince"(an administrator in a key position
who delivers lofty and ringing speeches to the faculty, coming
down on the "right side" of every issue, leaving the president to
handle the hot issues) will often find himself with a crown prince
at the next university. The president who has a quarrelsome and
unreasonable senate at one institution will, with surprising frequency, find the senate quarrelsome at the next. And the dean who
finds that students are hostile to him will seem to repeat that experience, even when he moves to an institution across the conti-

nent. These constancies exist not just because the problems facing campuses everywhere are much the same but because the interaction of a president with an academic community somehow makes him the parent of his own difficulties. In some subtle way, we, as administrators, seem to pick the problems that will afflict us.

A final note on this topic: It helps to have an administrative team that is well balanced, in terms of both personality characteristics and fields of preparation. Team styles enable such a group to profit from one another's strengths and to compensate weaknesses. The obvious adjustment to the personal styles and weaknesses of individual administrators by the campus is not so pejoratively apparent under these circumstances.

The Principle of "the More, the More" and "the Less, the Less." To an extent, there is a natural tendency for success to feed on success or failure on failure. If, by early spring, there are upsetting events which agitate the campus, surely there will be more by April. But if the campus remains relatively tranquil until the first of April, significant campus upsets are unlikely before finals—"the less, the less." If the president of the institution is honored by some campus group, other groups will join the parade. If, on the contrary, the president finds himself in difficulty with some major constituency, criticisms will surface from other quarters—"the more, the more."

This principle is familiar to fund raisers. A large gift from a well-known person is frequently a satisfactory kickoff for a fundraising campaign. If a dozen or two highly visible people in the community can be persuaded to make sizable gifts, so much the better. In the case of state institutions, when the legislature is generous with funds, the governor often seems to be similarly persuaded.

The implications of this principle are interesting. The administrator should be aware of the general climate of the campus. When things are going well, when the institution is viewed as moving in proper directions, the president or dean will have considerable support. Everyone loves a winner. A higher percentage of mistakes will be permitted. The president can take harder positions and press more rapidly for change. Very seldom do problems of a serious nature erupt when there is a rising barometer. The more constituent groups feel that things are going well, the more they minimize contradictions of that feeling and move with the tide. But when the barometer is falling, care should be taken not to make sudden moves. Criticisms will be sharper and more quickly brought forward. Ambiguous events will be interpreted negatively. More members of the academic community will be willing to "throw down" on an administrator.

The general principle to be observed is to move with and accelerate the upward sweep of the curve and to go slowly and attempt to reduce a downward trend when it appears. The most effective administrators, as I pointed out earlier, seem to sense these currents and adapt to them, whereas relatively less effective administrators seem to have a more static, nonorganismic model.

Resistance to Change

Universities can be incredibly tenacious in their counter-reactions to being shoved. When changes are initiated under forced draft, they may not stick. A member of the faculty at the University of Chicago in the 1960s once made the wry observation that the University was still in the process of unraveling the tapestry woven by Hutchins. Like an organism invaded by a foreign substance, institutions can spend incredible amounts of energy resisting and reworking decisions that are viewed as alien. At the most general level, a number of "strong" presidents have observed that over a period of time so many resistances developed to their actions and so many checks on presidential decision making were built into the machinery after something had been "accomplished" that, after a number of years, their freedom of movement was enormously restricted.

A most poignant awareness of the resisting character of universities is found in administrators' frequent complaints that their "orders" are being ignored. To put matters in perspective, we should recognize that university presidents and deans are not unique in such complaints. Such resistances are commonplace in almost every kind of organization, at least within a democratic society. Schlesinger (1958, p. 536) has observed of the national presidency: "The worst error a President can make is to assume the automatic implementation of his decisions. In certain respects, having able subordinates aggravates that problem, since strong personalities tend to have strong ideas of their own. Civil government operates by consent, not by command: the President's task, even within his own branch of government, is not to order but to lead. Students of public administration have never taken sufficient account of the capacity of lower levels of government to sabotage or defy even a masterful President."

Another example of resistance to orders comes from James McGregor Burns (1970, p. 223). Writing of the war years in the Roosevelt administration, Burns talks of the occasion in 1942 when Secretary Knox, with the approval of Roosevelt, had ordered the fleet into deep water to "fight the Japanese." After a few hours of steaming, the fleet had turned back. Knox asked Winston Churchill, who was on one of his periodic visits to Washington, "What would you do with your admiral in a case like this?" Churchill replied mildly that "it was dangerous to meddle with admirals when they say they can't do things. They have always got the weather or fuel or something to argue about." Schlesinger (1965, p. 423) refers to the same phenomenon in the Kennedy days: "The White House staff, in addition to offering the President independent comment on proposals from the departments, served as a means of discovering whether his instructions were being carried out. On occasions too frequent to record, the staff would have to say that State or Defense were not doing the things in one area or another they had been directed to do."

Of course this characteristic of organizations is not always viewed as a vice by the people offering the resistance. It is surprising how many times someone in a key position will describe with genuine satisfaction the way in which orders from the "boss" were resisted, with a good result, and why it was necessary to resist them. Jesse Jones, former chairman of the Reconstruction Corporation and secretary of commerce, commenting about his relationships with Franklin Roosevelt, said, "In the twelve years I worked for and with him, we never had an argument. We did not always see alike. If he asked me to do something which in my opinion we could not or should not do—and that happened only a few times—we just did not do it. For me that was the only way to operate without having a break with the President" (Jones and Edwards, 1951, p. 262). Jonathan Daniels (1946, pp. 31-32) seemed to feel that the necessity for ignoring presidential orders was so obvious that it did not even require an explanation. He stated, "Half of a President's suggestions, which theoretically carry the weight of orders, can be safely forgotten by a Cabinet member. And if the President asks about a suggestion a second time, he can be told that it is being investigated. If he asks a third time, a wise Cabinet officer will give him at least part of what he suggests. But only occasionally, except about the most important matters, do Presidents ever get around to asking three times."

University administrators possess no immunity from the tendency of people in organizations to resist orders. The problem, again, is seeing such resistance in a pathological, rather than a homeostatic, context. An illustration comes to mind. A president of my acquaintance asked the academic deans to develop a formula for assigning teaching loads to the faculty. No one particularly objected. Things just didn't get done. They drifted. The president became a little annoyed and began to push the deans. There were always reasons, always plausible excuses for delay. No one was a willing scoundrel. No one was exclusively responsible. And no one was obviously resisting. The president later reflected, "When there is that much resistance to some proposal I make, it is easy for me to forget that many decisions affect other people more than they affect me. It's easy to ignore the fact that sometimes people have better ideas than I do about decisions that will affect them." The same administrator also made the observation that, in retrospect, he realized that had he pushed for the implementation of the formula at that particular time, the campus would have blown up. Perhaps the resisters subliminally recognized this probability.

The implications of this resistive characteristic for administrative style are not that whenever orders are ignored, the entire matter should be dropped. But administrators should see resistance to orders as more than just the widespread distribution of original sin. Sometimes what is being observed is simply the other side of the dialectic. And thus an exploratory, problem-solving orientation is more in order than an attitude of offended majesty.

Implications of the Homeostatic View

Administrators, aware that the institution is richly counter-reactive to administrative action, recognize that cues are given at a great rate. To use an overworked term, *feedback* on the actions of administrators is in evidence everywhere. This is not to say that every squeak must be attended to or that each signal has the same significance as every other signal—just that messages exist about how constituents are responding. Emphatically, the university is not inert. An awareness of these reactive characteristics of campuses suggests that administrators need to be careful not to overcorrect the compass.

Dangers of Overcorrecting. The report reaches the president, in a tight budget year, that a junior faculty member has preempted a copying machine of one of the colleges for two full days to make copies of a small textbook for each member of his class so they won't have to "spend the money." Everyone goes cuckoo. A series of corrective measures are taken which are hard-jawed and puni-tive. The use of the copying machine must now be approved by the department chairman. It is then pointed out in a bitter ex-change of memos that there had, indeed, been a kind of watery approval from the department chairman for duplicating the book. So a decision is somehow made that since department chairmen cannot be fully trusted, a dean must countersign the departmental approval. An administrator complains that his office will be left uninformed of what has been approved, and the directive goes out that all approvals must be in quadruplicate so that relevant people may have a copy. A fairly sizable and costly system is set up to catch the half-dozen potential "nuts" who might abuse a copying ma-chine. A clear case of overkill. The better course? Call in the of-fending faculty member, explain matters, and invite him or her to mend their ways.

Another incident. It is the holiday season. A package breaks open in the campus mailroom, and a teddy bear tumbles out. Someone on the faculty or staff is using the university mailing priv-ilege to send out Christmas gifts. The alarm gong sounds. Many hours are consumed in trying to establish a tight security system that will still conform to federal laws of privacy. The faculty and staff begin to feel pushed and distrusted. Highly adrenalized speeches are made in the coffee room. Lawsuits are threatened for invasion of privacy. Academic freedom comes up for some discussion. And so the plot goes.

The extrapolation of this kind of incident into the constabulary view is discussed elsewhere in the book. Here I am not suggesting that administrators must be "pigeons." But they do not need to bend the entire world out of shape to avoid looking like pigeons, either. A wise jurist once observed, "Hard cases make bad law."

A final example: The university has a very bright treasurer. He stops one morning to leave his automobile to be repaired in a garage owned and operated by an old acquaintance close to the campus. The owner of the garage complains to the treasurer, "I don't know what I'm going to do. My mechanics are stealing me blind. They're carrying off all kinds of spare parts in their lunchboxes or under their sweaters." The treasurer asks, "Why don't you set up a parts department and hire a parts manager?" The garage owner snaps, "Because they're only stealing two thousand dollars a year, and a parts manager would cost me twelve!" Would that higher education could be so smart! How many have witnessed exercises costing thousands of dollars designed to catch one or two unsteady people in improper behavior, when simply calling in the people involved and telling them to behave would have handled the situation 90 percent of the time.

Dealing with Continuing Irritations. After considerable experience an administrator learns to trust the homeostatic tendencies of universities.* The realization that such trust is possible often comes first as a happy surprise when a newly appointed dean or president suddenly discovers that a great many problems solve

---

*This kind of trust may be responsible in part for one of William Rainey Harper's maxims of administration: "The president should never do today what by any possible means he can postpone until tomorrow." Harper warned that premature action was "the source of many more mistakes than procrastination" (Knight, 1940, p. 346). The Harper statement is so zany in its variance from the conventional bracing rhetoric of administrative writing, it catches the attention.

themselves if left alone. But there's a trap here. Administrators can sometimes neglect their part in the political dialectic processes of the campus because they fail to understand the limitations of these homeostatic tendencies. It is true that sometimes administrators rush in too soon to correct some problem or to defend themselves. The opposite mistake can occur when an administrator becomes too impressed with the capacity of the institution to solve its own problems.

In the following example, the problem was not self-correcting because it originated off-campus. (Besides, computers are notorious for not being self-correcting.) In a state university the checks for student financial aid were late because of a major hernia in the computer system in the state capital. Although there was vigorous complaint from students, administrators largely ignored the problem. They felt the problem was not of their making. They also felt that their innocence was obvious. In any event, they argued, the spring vacation was almost at hand and certainly the checks would be issued before the students returned to class. Some of the checks came over the holiday; some did not. By the time the students had returned to campus, a considerable movement of criticism was growing among the students. The administration still took the view that it was "unreasonable to get so excited about a problem that will soon be solved." Student leaders took the seeming lack of concern as symbolic of administrative indifference to students and their problems. Then other campus events that might otherwise have been trivial began to take on the proportions of minor disasters. For the next two or three weeks there was considerable bitching among administrators about how unjust the entire episode was. They tended to brush over the fact that they had an opportunity to capture the situation symbolically, to demonstrate concern and to see whether delivery of the checks could be accelerated.

Operating in a Process World. The world of university administration is a political/democratic world, but a world moderated and influenced by institutional metabolism. That metabolism demands of and imposes on administrators who are effective and successful a kind of satisfaction in process goals—a satisfaction with direction rather than with specific victories or particular tasks accomplished.

They see achievement in continual movement and change. In the homeostatic model administrators must learn to derive a sense of success from trends instead of fixed scenarios played out once and forever. The homeostatic administrative world is a balancing system of statement and counterstatement, pull-and-tug compromise, and long-term drifts up and down. Administration must be felt as this kind of experience. In addition to being a way of moving, it is a way of perceiving. The constant movement is not random. But neither are there any final solutions to problems. One solution becomes, in itself, a problem requiring another solution. Perfection is never reached.

This process is undoubtedly less comfortable than the abstract rhetoric reveals. I have often wondered, for example, why many experienced administrators attending workshops feel a mild sense of discomfort with case studies. When a discussion leader is presenting a case, periodic halts are called. The leader summarizes what has occurred. A "snapshot" is presented of the situation at the point of halt. The group is then asked what should be done. After alternatives are discussed, the leader describes what actually happened. The discussion continues. A new problem focus soon develops. Another halt is called. Such a procedure gives a spurious sensation of comfort and mastery. There is a feeling of time available, a feeling that problems come seriatim, a feeling of opportunities to exercise reason in a sure-footed way. The comfort is offset by the suspicion that the administrative world doesn't operate like that. Most administrators of experience want to ask more questions. What is the mood of the campus? What other problems are likely to "heat up" conductively as a result of decisions taken in this arena? How did this or that key individual in the cast of characters really feel? What was the look in his eyes? How will he feel later after reflection? Who is mad and how mad are they? Often such information is treated as marginally important in case-study discussions.

The world of administration moves fast. It *is* a process. Every part is connected to every other part, and every decision affects every other decision. The case-study method somehow never seems to be able to place enough emphasis on the attitude and flow that develops in the styles of most effective administrators. Again, good administrators develop a feel for the currents and eddies, a respect for what comes in on their antennae, an almost intuitive sense of what will work and what will not, what will be productive and what will be disastrous. There never seems to be a point at which to stop and say, "This is the way it happened," because it is always still happening.

Homeostasis and Political Behavior

The kinds of activities here described as homeostatic behavior merge gradually into more characteristically political behavior. The check-and-balance systems of democratic states have a homeostatic rationale. And relatively open democratic societies seem to have other tendencies to self-correction too. The wonder of Watergate is not that it occurred but that we could administer to ourselves such an incredible national enema in our pursuit of self-correction. The links between political behavior and the so-called homeostatic processes characteristic of universities are difficult to specify, and similarly unimportant that we cannot do so precisely. It is probably also unimportant that sharp artificial distinctions between them cannot be made. The homeostatic influences in a university probably operate less visibly than does more characteristically political behavior. Perhaps they have most impact in situations where the stakes do not seem to be so high and where the adjustments seem relatively painless. Clearly, political behavior is more noticeable when the competition for scarce resources, characteristic of the political arena, is pushing the agenda.

Five

———————⟋———————

Managing, Making Decisions, and the Presidential Role

Volumes have been written with titles like "The Management of the University." And I am not, of course, simply attempting to add to the list. Although this book deals with many of the topics covered in such volumes, its principal thrust does not fit the usual textbook categories. Nevertheless, certain administrative topics should be treated under traditional headings, and hence the title of this chapter and its contents.

Administration from the Top Down

An incident reported in the *Chronicle of Higher Education* (in Van Dyne, August 19, 1974, p. 4) illustrates the view that the best administration proceeds from the top down. For the present discussion, the precipitating incident of the controversy is unimportant. Suffice it to quote here the comments of the chairman of the board of Southwestern Michigan College in response to the episode: "They [the trustees] think it [the college] ought to be run from the top down—the people elect the trustees, the trustees set the policies, and the faculty and administrators carry them out. . . . A lot of colleges wouldn't be in the mess they are in if trustees had remembered that simple hierarchy of authority and had stood up to the demands of their faculties. . . . At a lot of these colleges the tail has been wagging the dog for years." He concluded, according to the *Chronicle* report: "The hired help have been running things . . . we've got to move to a situation where the dog wags the tail again."

The chancellor of a large state system of higher education stated the same point of view in more general terms: "I am drawing a conclusion based on history with which some of you may not agree—to the effect that human institutions are simply not operable in an effective way for very long periods of time without strong and responsible leadership. There are cycles in which this leadership is questioned, such as we are going through at the present time; and there are subsequent periods when authority is temporarily decentralized, but inevitably, in order to make human institutions work, they must return, and always have, to the concept of strong individual leadership, whatever the pattern of government in which it operates" (Dumke, 1973).

These two statements reflect the application to university governance of the classical view of administration held by Woodrow Wilson and applied, largely as a result of his efforts, to the United States public service. The theory has been a most influential one in this nation. Wilson's basic "reality" in politics rested on the assumptions that "there is always *a* center of power" (Ostrom, 1973, p. 24) and that "the more power is divided, the more irresponsible it becomes" (p. 25). Ostrom continues: "The science of administration, according to Wilson, was most fully developed by French and German scholars at the turn of the century. . . . in Prussia under Frederick the Great and Frederick William III and in France under Napoleon. . . . Monarchies and democracies may differ with respect to the political structures of their constitutions, but their administrative systems operate upon the same technical principles." Thus, "Wilson could conceive of a theory of democratic government but *not* a theory of *democratic administration*" (p. 27).

Taking a gloomy view of the Wilsonian-French-Prussian model of administration, Ostrom says, "The major task in the next decade will be to lay new foundations for the study of public administration" (p. 5). In support of this statement, he points out that attempted control measures in World War II were characterized by persistent failures because the principles of administration laid out in classic theory did not work. In fact the gap between theory and practice widened. The most devastating theoretical blow to the classical view, according to Ostrom, came from Herbert Simon in his study of *Administrative Behavior*. In this volume Simon rejects the classical principles of public administration as "little more than proverbs" (p. 7). Ostrom concludes, "The wartime experiences with civil and military administration were more congruent with the work of Elton Mayo and his colleagues . . . in the Western Electric experiment than with the work of Urwick and Gulick. The human relations aspect of organization appeared to have a greater effect on productivity then formal tables of organization" (pp. 6-7).

The analysts who point to a crisis in public administration as a result of the collapse of the traditional Wilsonian theories are finding support for their views among those who work every day at administering bureaucracies. Charles L. Schultze, budget director under President Eisenhower, testifying before the subcommittee on executive reorganization of the Senate Committee on Government Operations on June 29, 1967, stated: "This hierarchical concept of management, however valid in the usual situation, is of limited help in the unique problem we now confront. To manage the new social programs efficiently we must get many governmental units—all of which have equal status—to work together on a single project without anyone being considered the 'boss' of the others. We have to develop the managerial techniques of voluntary cooperation—and that is much tougher than the other way of having people told what they are to do."

If it is true that classical models of centralized hierarchical administration have not worked well for the public service since at least World War II, it is even more true that such models have not worked well as a guiding philosophy for administering universities. A kind of schizophrenia develops in institutions where system-headquarters administrators or trustees pay lip service to a classical, hierarchical philosophy while campus administrators are forced to develop more effective, "masked" styles in order to get the job done, styles that do not accord with the rhetoric of traditional administration.[7]

Even those removed from day-to-day campus administrative problems often sense that there are some difficulties with the "down from the top" concept. For one thing, the appropriate level of final authority in the classical structure tends to drift upward. Students obviously cannot be trusted to manage their own affairs; therefore, decisions affecting them should be in the hands of the faculty and administration. At a somewhat higher level in the pyramid, it is felt that presidents of universities are a trace unreliable. The authority for final and crisp decision making on truly important matters thus tends to find its way into the hands of a chancellor. Sometimes boards of trustees come to distrust the chancellor and feel that they should have a greater say in decisions. In state institutions legislators, in turn, tend to view trustees as feckless or unreliable and to take the position that important matters are best left to them. Governors tend to look at legislators with a slight squint. And federal bureaucrats from their own perspective are increasingly unimpressed with the way states manage their educational affairs, an attitude that may account for their increasing involvement in decision making in public higher education.

The restlessness and uneasiness of public administration theorists and practitioners about traditional models are finally beginning to spread in the field of higher education. The Carnegie Commission (1973) has expressed strong reservations about the centralized coordination and controlling mechanisms that have grown out of the application of "administration from the top down" views of higher educational management. Other evidence is provided by remarks such as John Corson's: "State and federal coordinators-controllers must be aware that a dynamic, innovative faculty can be reduced to the pulp of time-serving bureaucracy by remote 'coordination' " (Ikenberry, 1974, p. 23). And many effective campus administrators share his cynicism.[7]

Carried to an extreme, the notion of control from the top down can even participate in the elaborate rationalizations and cosmologies of authoritarianism. Although the intention of such an arrangement is efficiency and not despotism, classical administration is justified most consistently by a distrust of people and their ability to manage their own affairs wisely. For those required to work under the direction of people removed from the problem who have been forced unaware into a cosmology of "superior wisdom," the end result may indeed feel like tyranny. Perhaps, then, one is not completely out of touch with reality to suggest, even though it is hard counsel, that Harvey Wheeler's dictum (1970, p. 6) may have some relevance. Wheeler contends that "democracy has always drawn its meaning from the specific type of despotism it was designed to counteract. The common fact is that democratic forces are regularly called forth in opposition to despotism."

Likewise, the effectiveness of democratic political administrative styles on campuses may be partly related to reactions to the top-down arrangements in force in many areas of higher education today. The reason why these reactions and the disequilibriums occasioned by them are not more frequently noticed is that the top-down rhetoric is right. This kind of administration deals in tough talk and hard-line pronouncements. And also the real problems are not better publicized because of a bias in reporting. Whenever some national commission studies the effectiveness with which higher education is operating, it never asks the foot soldiers how the system is working. Usually the chancellor, president, vice-chancellor, or chairman of the board of trustees is asked to comment. For a variety of reasons that need no elaboration here, the reports tend to be rather complimentary of the entire operation, with perhaps a little muttering about the "unsteady" character of present-day students and the "unworldly and contentious" characteristics of faculty. The amount of behind-the-scenes maneuvering, foot dragging, wasted effort, fuming obfuscation and delay, the time spent in unsuccessful constabulary efforts to make a system work on an unsatisfactory model is not calculated.

It is a difficult thing to understand how administrative arrangements staffed by individuals as dedicated, conscientious, and intelligent as those in any other group could result in problems. How does one get a diseased system when the people who run it are no more wicked, even if no more virtuous, than those who experience the results of hierarchical structures as afflictions and diseases? An example will supply at least an instance of how such difficulties arise. David Mathews, secretary of the Department of Health, Education and Welfare under President Ford, recounts the following incident:

> I was sitting in the office reviewing a group of regulations we were about to promulgate. In one case, I was told that a particular regulation had to be published in the *Federal Register*. This regulation was going to make certain distinctions between persons applying for some education grants, so that some would be able to get them while others would not. Under the authorizing statute both groups would have had an equal shot, but because there are so many applicants and it is necessary to make judgments between them in spending a limited amount of money, the Department was by this regulation establishing criteria for funding.
>
> I did not have great difficulty with this. What I did have difficulty with was that I was being asked to publish the regulation and make it immediately effective without any opportunity for the affected public to comment on it or to say what it thought about it.
>
> While I could appreciate the fact that the Department is an administrative body, I was still puzzled by this proposal. I said, "It occurs to me that since we—the federal government—had been the enforcers of due process, it will appear, at best, confusing to many people if we ourselves violate the principle. It seems to me that the public will sooner or later demand that the champions of due process be themselves due in their own processes" [Mathews and Heard, 1976].

The problem seems to be the model used, rather than the people involved. The top-down orientation is susceptible to the notion that the rules are designed for those below the decision maker in the pyramid. Those higher up are assumed to be a different class of people who do not need to be so closely controlled. Those who make the rules make them for others, not themselves.

At this point, I hear the questions: "Is yours an unspoken opposition to all systems of higher education or, indeed, all forms of bureaucracy?" "Isn't it true that some things can be better done by a central office of a system than by individual campuses competing with one another?" "Isn't it true that bureaucracies exist for defensible and functional reasons, even though they are imperfect?" The answer is yes to each of these questions. The problems do not inhere in the existence of a structure or bureaucracy, per se, although large and removed bureaucracies are somewhat predisposed to the infirmities here discussed. The problems derive from an improper philosophy of administration and attitudes toward people in organizations. Good management can exist in large systems and in state bureaucracies. Sound philosophies can influence the operations of both. All virtue does not reside in smallness or in autonomy.

The Constabulary View

The idea that administration is best when it proceeds from the top down nurtures the growth of what I call the constabulary view (Walker, 1976). Since centers of administration that are removed from the day-to-day problems tend to spawn rules and regulations that are unrealistic, unworkable, or unjust in the minds of those who must live with them, such rules and regulations are frequently evaded, often very imaginatively. Sometimes they are the source of merriment within the university. Always they are the source of cynicism. The result, of course, is a great effort "topside" to police the operation. From this need for police activity comes the constabulary perspective.

In pyramidal, highly organized structures the administrative distortions that result from perpetually trying to get "control" can become a raging disease. So every administrator must decide sometime early in the game how much of his or her time will be spent as a constable. The game of "catch 'em" is never ending. Police activity can become a full-time job. Sometimes it's the easiest kind of administration to do, not in terms of results, but because the agenda is clear, strategies are relatively few and clean cut, and at least everyone understands what is going on. Ambiguity concerning the administrative role is reduced.

There are three reasons why, in my view, the most effective administrators tend to avoid playing constable as much as possible. One, it is ineffective. An academic community is stuffed with able people. If the name of the game becomes to outwit authority, that game can be played exceedingly well by people of high intelligence and motivation. Indeed, it can be played with amazing success by people of average intelligence and average motivation. Generally speaking and on balance, the game of cops and robbers simply doesn't work on campus.

The second reason is not generally stressed: constabulary activity is expensive. The expense is most obvious in the pyramiding costs of central systems which attempt to actually manage, rather than coordinate, the operation of several institutions. When unrealistic and clumsy rules are resisted, central headquarters appoints constables to visit the campus and find out why the rules are not being followed. After two or three careful briefing sessions, the constables frequently decide "the rule won't work." To which the response in one form or another is "Exactly. Why don't you go for coffee?" Those in authority notice that the constables are sloughing and send in a team of auditors to discover the reasons. The auditors too find themselves taken into camp by reality. Their reports are equivocal and unsatisfying to top authorities. A team of auditors from another branch of central headquarters or from another state agency follows. The costs mount and mount, and somehow the expenses seem reasonable.

There's a third and more subtle reason why the most effective administrators tend to avoid giving too much effort to the policeman role. It subtly poisons the working climate of an institution because it assumes that people are bad and must be watched and controlled, that if they are left to their own impulses, they will surrender ultimately to exorbitant mischief. The fabric of trust begins to fray, people work with less enthusiasm and less appetite, and the juices begin to dry up.

The watcher psychology creates the derivative fear that people will "get away with something." Why is this bad? Because if they "get away with something" they will learn that it is possible to circumvent the watchers and "get away" with even more; they will learn "bad" lessons. The need becomes not only to catch people in misbehavior but to head them off from the possibility of misbehavior. This psychology pursued to its ultimate end stimulates unreasonably aggressive behaviors throughout the organization. Incredible amounts of time and energy are spent in preventing things from "going wrong," time and energy that otherwise might be used in more productive endeavor. Gradually a sense of direction is lost. Accountability comes to mean obedience.

It's easy for any organization to drift into the practice of spending great amounts of time trying to control people. A case in point. On a university campus located in a rural area, prime parking places in paved parking lots were tight, but generally speaking there were enough slots for everyone, even though many of the spaces were not close to classes. Parking stickers were provided, primarily to identify off-campus cars and to give a little preferred parking to people who, for some reason, were judged to have a need for preferment. Parking citations were issued only to people who were rather obviously and outrageously interfering with the rights of others. Money from the parking tickets went to the scholarship fund. One year there were some shifts in parking assignments. A lot was set aside for people in the administration building who had to come and go with some frequency, for elderly people, and for the handicapped. Even though no aggravated problem resulted from this change the campus chief of security somehow got the wrong idea. He issued a tough memorandum to the campus stating that anyone violating the parking rules would be towed away. His action was unwise for at least a couple of reasons. In the first place, there was no way that towing could be practically carried out. The university did not own a tow truck and the nearest one was several miles away. In the second place, the only justification that could be given for this suddenly hard-line view was that "people have to obey the rules."

The constabulary view makes the question of "who is responsible" a critical issue. The president of a large urban university describes an incident that shows how "matters can get off the track."

> On the first real day of spring, two beautiful trees in the infancy of bloom are chopped down to make room for cars to turn down a campus driveway. Everybody is outraged. Students pack into my office to tell me about it. A few are hysterical and crying. I leave my office and walk over to the little grass plot—there is so little green on our campus—to see a man with a small hand powersaw, cleaning and stacking up the milk-white wood into neat piles.

A crowd of some two hundred students and faculty stand around and hiss me as I break through the circle to speak to him. "Man, am I glad you're here. They're ready to crucify me." It turns out he is not employed by the university. He works for a local contractor. I could never find out who was responsible: the landscape artist who designed the new plot with poodle hedges, or his boss, the landscape architect; the director of planning, or his boss, the head of the physical plant; the vice president for management and finance, the university building committee, the executive vice president the committee reports to. . . . When I called them all together they numbered twenty, and they were innocents all. All of us. Bureaucracies are beautiful mechanisms for the evasion of responsibility and guilt [Bonham, 1977, pp. 160–161].

This exercise illustrates that the constabulary view, regardless of who practices it, is indeed (1) ineffective—the president never found the villain, (2) expensive—think of the cost of gathering twenty administrators to decide who was responsible, and (3) negative in its effect on the climate of the organization. After all is said and done, I wonder what the president would have done if someone had stepped forward and confessed to the crime. Fired him? Reprimanded him? Would that have prevented someone else from making the same mistake? The energy of the president and others involved would have been much better spent on deciding how to avoid similar incidents in the future and how to have more trees on campus. Obviously, there was a deep concern for trees, so why not react to the situation positively?

Actually, probably no single person could step forward and take responsibility because the decision was the result of a series of acquiescences, minor errors in judgment, and assumptions made by numerous people. Perhaps the reason it is difficult to fix responsibility in large organizations is that it really *is* difficult to fix responsibility. We do indeed live in an interdependent and process world. We are both accomplices and colleagues of one another. And I am not certain this situation is entirely perverse. In the real social-administrative milieu, with all its complexities, the person who needs a tidy administration with neat closures and with a cast of clearly identified villains and heroes will not fare well.

The Presidential Role

Though notes on the role of the president have been scattered explicitly and by clear implication through the preceding pages, it is appropriate, at this point, to discuss some of his or her additional responsibilities. This is a difficult section of the book to write. It may also be hardest for administrators to receive and to think about. It is difficult, in this arena above all, to sort out what we as administrators really believe about administration from what we think we ought to believe. Many books have been written about the university presidency, yet there is a surprisingly small supply of material that is actually helpful to presidents in resolving day-to-day dilemmas. I am not talking about a cookbook; I am talking about writing that presents a realistic feel for the mixmaster challenges of a presidential week. I believe the gap in the writing is due not to indolence or indifference on the part of administrators but to three influences: one, the high specific gravity of personal experience in the absence of a consistent perspective; two, the concept of the heroic university presidency; and three, the history of the university itself.

The Absence of Realistic Theories. There are few tournament-level theories in the arena of practical administration. Since we have no sophisticated and generally shared concepts of how administration actually works, we accord exalted status to our own experiences. We are guilty of what Jim March has referred to as "superstitious learning." A regularity in the operation comes to our attention, an administrative maneuver is "successful," and, bingo, we have a principle. We sound like imbecile owls.

In the absence of appropriate and realistic theory, we are at a loss to coherently explain the effectiveness of seemingly different administrative styles. We retreat to clichés: "Well, different administrative styles work for different people." The statement is often accompanied by a shrug, as if to say, with Mark Twain, "Why shouldn't life be stranger than fiction? Fiction has to make sense."

The Concept of the Heroic University Presidency. As I pointed out earlier, university presidents, along with other high-status symbolic leaders in the society, tend to see their actions as heroic. And since much of the writing about university administrations is done by presidents or former presidents, the heroic bias is introduced into their remembering. They are not being dishonest. It is just that they are looking at their experiences through available lenses. Kierkegaard was unquestionably right in his view that though life must be lived forward, it can only be understood backward. Biases in the backward look are inevitable. In writing about presidential experience after the fact, the author generally glosses over the hand-over-hand pragmatic feeling of day-to-day administration: ambiguities drop out; vacillations disappear; clumsiness is smoothed over.

Of course presidents are not uniquely wicked in the tendency to egotistically rosy reporting. The egos of motion-picture actors are notoriously bulky too. Someone once remarked, for instance, that "Orson Welles expects applause when he gets out of the bathtub." But we're not just talking about the fact that "human nature is very prevalent." The responsibility for giving heroic proportions to the activities of public figures belongs also to the society at large. We need to make heroes of those on whom we depend. Prominent people, from their side of the equation, may tend to accept heroic definitions of their actions to reduce their own feelings of anxiety and ambiguity. It is possible that because of the *quid pro quo* character of the Protestant ethic, anyone in the society reaching an ambiguous pinnacle position must find reasons for his or her success or else bear an uncomfortable burden of guilt.

The tendency of leaders to accept heroic perceptions of themselves can be subtly corrupting of presidential perspective. The president's jokes are vastly appreciated. Her little witticisms are treasured and repeated, her opinion deferred to. My father, a wise administrator and academic, once observed, "Flattery is like perfume. It's all right to sniff it, but it is not to be swallowed." It is difficult, however, for presidents to resist the tendency to think of themselves as really as brilliant as the behavior of others toward them would seem to indicate that they are. When a president does succumb to peacock fever, it can be bad news for everyone in the institution, including the president.

Related to the distorting effect of the image of the heroic presidency is the undue weight given to the pronouncements of presidents of large and prestigious universities. We tend to admire highly a person who manages a sizable enterprise, but in fact such an administrator may have a particularly inaccurate picture of reality. For one thing, the president of a large institution may very easily become separated from intimate personal contact with the faculty and students. Surrounded by a good-sized personal staff, the president is often shielded from awareness of intemperate criticism, as well as from knowing his constituents' problems. And thus his office may become a hall of mirrors. Those around the president adjust homeostatically to presidential style. Furthermore, the several layers of administrative personnel between the president and the faculty and students provide filters which remove the unworkable or unreasonable elements of his decisions. The fact that these decisions are subtly changed often does not reach his attention. So everything that the president does seems to work. Nevertheless, when such a president uncritically retreats to stereotyped beliefs and pronouncements about university administration, other presidents on pedestals of lesser eminence hear the pronouncements of the emperor and marvel well. They believe they are observing the validation of traditional administrative philosophy. But they may not be observing what a hands-on administrator does to succeed. What they may, in fact, be seeing is how a homeostatic administrative system works to make an unrealistic philosophy of administration succeed.

It is probable that every book written by administrators, including this one, will be distorted in some of its paragraphs, pages, or even chapters by the heroic-administrator bias in perception.

The History of the University as an Impediment to Realistic Views of Administration. At the time of their establishment, universities were regarded as keeping-places for the young. It was not unusual for students to enroll in universities at thirteen or fourteen years of age, and sometimes even younger. At that time, the well-known *in loco parentis* role was assumed by universities, which were expected to monitor not only the intellectual development of students but their lives in general. How successfully these monitoring functions were performed is debatable. Nevertheless, the perception of the university as a keeping-place for the immature is still influential. The ideal administrative model for such an institution, it would seem, would be somehow familial or custodial.

In spite of the fact that students on many urban campuses

now average twenty or twenty-one years of age, and that in most states eighteen is regarded as the age of majority, universities are still seen as aggregations of the immature for another reason. Maturity, in most societies, including our own, is a matter more of economics than of hormones. An individual is regarded as mature in most cultures not when sexual procreation is possible but when economic independence has been established. Most students are not regarded by the society as economically independent in the full adult sense.

The recent history of university campuses has also contributed to biases in favor of custodial and hierarchical models of campus management. The disruptions of the sixties, as we have seen, created strong negative feelings toward universities among influential constituencies. Campuses came to be regarded as rather chaotic and recalcitrant enterprises, expensive and poorly managed, staffed with feckless faculties badly in need of masters, and attended by thin-blooded students whose egocentric, cultish, and disruptive behaviors could only be partly salvaged by characterizing them as immature.

During these troubled days, the equally stereotyped views of the university held by radical student leaders were no improvement. Many leaders of campus protest saw the university as an organized hierarchy of privilege and power, with subtle ways of giving the impression of dispersed authority in order to deceive frustrated students.

Finally, the campus difficulties of the sixties seemed to call forth our need as a people for intentionality in the institutions that serve us. We are pragmatists. We like to see things move and change. And we have strong needs to feel that we can direct such change. Traditional ideas about how the universities ought to work satisfy such needs.

Such biases, even though they are held by others, exert a subtly distorting effect on the perceptions of administrators. Accordingly, I will try in the following discussion to present an altered and, I hope, realistic perspective of the office of the president by analyzing several of the myths or misconceptions about it. My object is not to be simply a proctoring thorn so much as to remove some of the more obvious attitudinal barriers to a more realistic conception of presidential responsibilities. I begin the considera-

tion of these several topics with a careful look at the notion that
one of the most important responsibilities of a president is to be
the horizon planner for the university.

The President as Long-Term Planner and Master Architect. It is
a well-seated piece of administrative wisdom or mythology that the
"best" presidents spend most of their time looking down the long
vistas of the future into which their institutions will move in response to their vision and at their command. The view of the university as the shadow of a strong president is unrealistic now, however, if indeed it was ever accurate. The picture of the president
as the guiding genius behind all consecutive gains and directional
purpose in an institution is based on an unreal perception of how
campuses function. Of course, the president is and should be an
important part of the process of change. But campuses simply do
not change permanently in response to the decisions and the will
of a single person.

The more administratively agile, or perhaps the more self-
deluding, presidents may believe they are the unilateral movers
and shakers of the institution. They are able to maintain this mythology because it is possible, unaware, to take advantage of what
has happened at an institution. The president, after the fact, may
then declare the result to be what he or she had in mind all the
time. Alternatively, a president may simply have intuited the way
in which the institution was evolving and declared that agenda to
be his future program. On rare occasions I have even seen a president who, having started out in a totally different direction, finds
that indeed "life is what happens to you while you are planning."
Events sharply contradict the wisdom and feasibility of what the
president had in mind. Occasionally, it is possible for even such as
these to be convinced that the actual course of events as played out
is what was in the presidential consciousness all the while.

Again, this is not to say that presidential planning is not a
factor in fixing the direction of an institution. It is. But when such
planning is idiosyncratic, it is at best an influential factor in a dialectic process. The deeper societal and institutional forces operating on the university transcend the influence of such schemes.

The ultimate penalty for self-delusion, in this matter, is isolation from the real world. I have known one or two university

presidents who seemed to be so caught up in the majesty and the grandeur of their planning that they had, indeed, become isolated. They seemed to me to be moving hand puppets in a narcissistic charade that was largely ignored by the rest of the university. When a president tells me that he spends the greater part of his time thinking the big thoughts and ideas and conjuring the long-range vision, I'm troubled by the unworthy suspicion that I may be dealing with a nitwit, an ineffective administrator that people have walled off, while someone else gets the actual job of administration done.

I have considerable sympathy for the view held by such people as Alan Nevins, the Pultizer-prize-winning historian (1962), and John Rehfus, the political scientist, that significant change in major institutions of the society, including the university, results for the most part from outside pressures and not from inside decisions (Rehfuss, 1973, p. 230). I've also pledged considerable allegiance to Cohen and March's view that the university "appears to operate on a variety of inconsistent and ill-defined preferences. . . . It discovers preferences through action more often than it acts on the basis of preferences" (1974, p. 3). I am also struck with the embarrassing honesty of their statement that "almost any educated person can deliver a lecture entitled 'The Goals of the University.' Almost no one will listen to the lecture voluntarily" (p. 195).

I set these observations off against the apparently real need for people in academic institutions to engage in long-range planning. Perhaps they do it in an attempt to establish symbolic unity on a campus. Or perhaps the process reduces personal ambiguity and mitigates the feeling of uncertainty about the future. But I strongly suspect that the importance of long-range planning lies in its existence rather than in its effect on the institution. Its impact on people may be significant—there is some detritus of satisfaction deposited in the soul of the individuals who have been involved in such an effort—even though it simply affirms and emphasizes an external reality or else gets ignored.

These comments should not be taken to mean that a president should have no sense of direction. In the best presidents that sense of direction and of values derives from an appreciation of the potentialities inherent in the situation. It is not superimposed, as an alien presence; nor do the best administrators I have known feel that they are single-handedly directing the future course of events for the campus.

A final thought on long-range planning. Sometimes I have cross-examined those presidents who maintain "the principal job of the president of an institution is long-range planning." I have asked, "Just exactly what do you mean by long-range planning?" The answers are surprisingly variable. Sometimes what is really meant is a kind of a negative—to wit, the president should stay out of the day-to-day operation. He or she should be above the battle, should have a rather lofty and removed perspective, be impartial, not get involved in the pulley-hauley, the day-to-day nit picking and the problem solving. If this is all that is meant, I can concur entirely. The president who is involved in detail because of an inability to delegate, or because of an overweening sense that the job will not be done properly unless he does it, is more frequently than not a problem president.

Innovation and the President. Innovation is an extraordinarily sensitive issue on most campuses. Seasoned administrators sometimes confess to a trace of cynicism when they recognize the symbolic and political loadings that the topic acquires. They even confess to feeling that those campuses, or even those departments, that are heavily into the rhetoric of innovation are heavily into the *rhetoric* of innovation. Some campuses pride themselves on being innovative, but outside observers find it very difficult to see anything that is not pretty "old hat." Other campuses seem indifferent to the rhetoric and symbolism, yet manage to put some rather unusual ideas and programs into operation without much fanfare.

Thus, the topic of innovation is difficult to deal with. For one thing, *innovation,* like *excellence,* is a sliding word with different meanings to different people. Using the term in its broadest sense, I believe that universities change only as a result of outside pressures, as I said earlier. The university is not unique in this regard. Consequently, the notion of many in higher education that universities provide the leadership in major social changes is probably a fantasy. But universities have nevertheless been among the most responsive of major social institutions in reacting to societal demands for change—the seismic shifts in higher education following World War II being the most dramatic example in recent times.

Where does the president fit in this situation? Whether it is true or not that presidents are seldom innovators, the role of the president in innovation is probably most effective when it is indirect. Earl J. McGrath (1967, p. 11) quotes Clark Kerr as having remarked, "Innovations sometimes succeed best when they have no obvious author." McGrath also reports that while he was studying the administration of foreign universities for the Ford Foundation he once asked the vice chancellor of Oxford University whether, when he saw a need for a desirable change in the policies of the university, he would present his idea directly to the faculty. After a moment's hesitation, the vice chancellor replied, "Good Lord, no. Nothing would kill the idea more quickly." President Ernest Hopkins of Dartmouth is cited as a master of the technique of attributing to others ideas that he wished to put into operation.

McGrath also comments in some detail on a study by Richard H. Davis of the University of Chicago, who analyzed two Midwestern liberal arts colleges. He "examined the differences between one of the least innovative colleges belonging to the North Central Association and one of the most innovative. At first he wondered if the faculty at the tradition-bound college was simply unaware of educational developments elsewhere in the country, but he found no differences between the two in terms of their knowledge of current educational experimentation. Nor did he find any significant differences between the two faculties on psychological measures of conservatism" (p. 13). Davis found that the faculty members of both institutions thought of the president as innovative. But at the less innovative campus, the president "was seen as *proposing* most innovations." Whereas the more successful innovator accomplished more because he was able "to promote an openness to innovation so that faculty members would feel free to initiate or to consider a proposed change; second, he was available for consultation with faculty members, shared his ideas freely with an interested member, and did not oppose any educational program or practice an innovator proposed; and third, he supported a set of norms that assumed the faculty's participation in the governance of the institution" (p. 13). Davis concluded that the leadership style of the president was highly related to the success or failure of innovative programs.

The role of the president or other administrator need not always be limited to that of fertilizer of the soil. When administrative egos are not too bulky, and good ideas can be accepted from the faculty and students, the counterreactive tendency of academic communities can be used constructively to stimulate the university to productive and necessary change.

An illustration may help. A university badly needs some explicitly stated criteria for promotion. After some months of debate and inconclusive attempts to create a set of standards, one of the deans develops and proposes a list. The faculty is immediately galvanized into action. A number of student leaders become concerned. A faculty committee proposes its own list of criteria. It is, incidentally, probably a slightly better formulation than the one originally developed by the dean. There are a few "political" items on the list, however, probably put there for tactical advantage—at least this is the interpretation given by some administrators. A series of meetings is called. Some disagreements are resolved and a final plan is negotiated, a plan to which more people are committed because of their involvement in the satellite discussions and arguments.

In another instance, an innovative administrator develops a plan for a new program and proposes it to the university curriculum committee. There is immediately considerable reaction and unhappiness. Where will the resources come from? Who will review new faculty appointments before they are made? Should not the proposal for the new program have originated in one of the established departments? Cannot the need for the new program be met better by simply adding courses to two or three existing departments? Counterproposals surface from the faculty and go forward to the administration. So it goes.

The nostalgic, who may read the preceding paragraph with a rueful shake of the head and a feeling of regret for the "good old days" when presidents could, indeed, "innovate," would do well to remember some comments by William Rainey Harper in a memorandum dated 1904 and found in his files after his death: "When all has been said, the limitations on the college president, even when he has the greatest freedom of action, are very great. . . . In educational policy he must be in accord with his colleagues. If he cannot persuade them to adopt his views, he must go with them. It is absurd to suppose that any president, however strong or willful he may be, can force a faculty made up of great leaders of thought to do his will. The president, if he has the power of veto, may stand in the way of progress, but he cannot secure forward movement except with the cooperation of those with whom he is associated" (Harper, 1938, p. 8).

McGrath has further advice, in his quotations from Robert Hutchins, for the skeptic who feels that Hutchins, perhaps alone, remained an exception to the rule. Hutchins remarked:

> I now think that my lack of patience was one of my principal disqualifications as an administrator . . . It is one thing to get things done. It is another to make them last. I was interested in effecting permanent improvements in American education, not in keeping the University of Chicago in an uproar. I should have known that the existence of a large and embittered minority, which felt that fundamental alterations of the University and its program had been pushed through without consideration of its point of view, destined such alterations to endure only until the minority could muster the strength to become the majority. The example of the College of Cardinals, who, I understand, never decide anything unless the vote is unanimous, and of the Quakers, who continue their discussion until consensus is reached, suggests the procedure that makes durability likely. . . . I believe I should have done the same thing with the faculty representatives, who, under the constitution of the University of Chicago, have final power over all educational changes. If I had, I would have accomplished fewer things, but they might have survived longer [quoted in McGrath, 1967, pp. 8–9].

The President as Decision Maker. Decision making is sometimes referred to as the heart of the administrative process. If decisions are conceived as discrete events that can be taken one at a time in a series, then it is difficult to believe that such decision making is central to university administration. There is a kind of chaining effect in university decision making that gives it an interrelated and organic feel; and furthermore, that interrelatedness frequently exists in a political ambience.

Graham T. Allison (1969) has contributed a seminal article to the literature on decision making at the national level in his study of the Cuban missile crisis. It has relevance also, it seems to me, for campuses. After examining a number of models of how decisions are made in the public arena, he defends a "bureaucratic politics paradigm."

> My primary source [for this paradigm] is the model implicit in the work of Richard E. Neustadt, though his concentration on presidential action has been generalized to a concern with policy as the outcome of political bargaining among a number of independent players, the president amounting to no more than a "super power" among many lesser but considerable powers. As Warner Schilling argues, the substantive problems are of such inordinate difficulty that uncertainties and differences with regard to goals, alternatives, and consequences are inevitable. This necessitates what Roger Hilsman describes as the process of conflict and consensus building. The techniques employed in this process often resemble those used in legislative assemblies [1969, p. 708].

Allison could be speaking of decision making on a campus rather than the decisions of national government when he refers to such decisions and actions as

> essentially intranational political outcomes: outcomes in the sense that what happens is not chosen as a solution to a problem but rather results from compromise, coalition, competition, and confusion among government officials who see different faces of an issue; political in the sense that the activity from which the outcomes emerge is best characterized as bargaining. Following Wittgenstein's use of the concept of a "game," national behavior in international affairs can be conceived as outcomes of intricate and subtle, simultaneous, overlapping games among players located in positions, the hierarchical arrangement of which constitutes the government. These games proceed neither at random nor at leisure. Regular channels struc-

ture the game. Deadlines force issues to the attention of
busy players. The moves in the chess game are thus to be
explained in terms of the bargaining among players with
separate and unequal power over particular pieces and with
separable objectives in distinguishable sub-games [1969, p.
708].

If decision making is viewed in this larger context but in
political terms, rather than in game-theory terms, then one can
argue that decision making is central to the administrative effort
even on campuses. But the pragmatic requirements of the president's position call for him or her to be something broader than
a decision maker—a problem solver (that phrase again). Problem
solving consists not only of being "a part of outcomes" or even of
being "a super power among lesser, but considerable powers." It
consists of interpreting, pulling people in from the periphery and
operating within the interstices of bargaining, compromising and
decision making to see that things somehow work. Perhaps I am
quibbling, but the distinction between decision making and problem solving seems important enough to be remarked. Decision
making when applied to campus administration seems to connote
a choice between unsatisfactory solutions with the implication being
that someone is going to be unhappy and someone has to take the
heat. The view seems to be that conflict is inevitable. Certainly conflict often occurs even when the problem-solving model is applied.
The problem-solving style, however, operates more with the view
that many problems can be resolved to the mutual satisfaction of
the people affected or else that an approach can be made that is
close enough to this goal that at least there is acceptance. Again
the texture and feel is different. The problem-solving definition
of presidential responsibility is more realistic than the hierarchical
stereotype of the president as the master decision maker for the
organization. Presidents do, of course, make decisions in the traditional sense. The process deserves discussion. Most effective administrators I have observed think of themselves not as responsible
for making every decision but as presiding over a process. Their
job, as they see it, is to ensure that decisions are in fact made, and
within appropriate time limits. They also pay attention to the procedures by which such decisions are made and the constituencies
represented in arriving at those decisions. Effective presidents view

the fact that the decisions were made consultatively, sometimes raggedly, and often with a team, as no rebuke to the final result.

Once more, the style I am advocating in this book does not demand that all decisions be consensual. As I mentioned elsewhere, sometimes the president can advance the dialectic by saying: "Fine, we seem to have come as far as we can together. All the alternatives that we can see have been explored. Since there is no agreement, I'm assuming you wish me to make the decision. This is your last chance. . . ." Again, the point should be emphasized that the president cannot escape responsibility for the decision, however it is arrived at. Presidential action of this sort may renew the dialectic process. If not, so be it. The fact that the group reaches an impasse probably signals that consent, if not approval, has been given. Also, I'm not suggesting that every decision requires a group meeting: there is a process of consensus creation, consensus seeking, and consensus affirming that goes on with or without group meetings. If a consensus is latently present, a presidential decision can call it forth and pin it down.

The rhetoric about decision making tends to obscure the conditional quality of many decisions made by effective administrators. Reality isn't brittle enough for final, absolute, no-compromise, no-retreat decisions. Yet the identification of decisions as "conditional" sounds wishy-washy when judged by traditional models. The concept is practically never discussed. In our stereotype, we know how "top-notch," "high-powered," "get the job done" executives make decisions. Right? They spend reasonable amounts of time in consultation. They gather whatever information is available. They weigh the pros and cons of the questions before them. They announce their anticipated decision in advance to give people a chance to make final and reasonable repair. Then, they take their shot. After that, people, including the decision maker, must live with the decision. If things don't turn out right, we just take the lashes. Right? Not always. Some presidential decisions may seem to follow that scenario fairly closely. Suppose, however, that not all the facts were available when the decision was made, either because someone practiced the art of incomplete disclosure or because new facts have come to light. Or suppose the situation at the institution has changed so much since the decision that a totally different campus chemistry now exists. Or what if the

emotional reaction of people affected by the decision is extreme—
a reaction not calculated in making the decision? What then? The
more effective administrators I have watched may indulge in some
rodomontade, but they often convene another meeting to say, in
one way or another, "We miscalculated on this one. We didn't have
all the facts, and we didn't realistically anticipate community reaction. Let's go back and do it over again." In my mind, I can hear
someone saying, "That shouldn't happen. There isn't a single
tough decision that everyone will agree with. Someone is always
going to be unhappy. If people discover that it's possible to reopen
issues, nothing will ever get decided. We'll be battered for a re-
versal on every decision." There is another objection. "No administrator will want to stick his or her neck out for fear he will get it
broken." In my experience, such fears are exaggerated to the point
of caricature. In the early days of a new president's tenure, maneuvering understandably goes on. There will be difficulties of the
type just described, but these will arise with or without "conditional
decision making." They come with the territory. When administrators develop a problem-solving orientation with no solution becoming part of anyone's skin, the tone of the enterprise changes.
Administrators begin to come in and say, "I know I recommended
this decision to you, but the situation is more complicated than I
thought. Maybe we had better go back and look at it again."

One benefit of the conditional-decision-making attitude is
that people can't simply push administrators into a decision and
then stand back and watch them fight to make it stick. Everyone
stays on board until the problem is solved. The object is to get good
solutions to problems, not to protect egos. Conditional decision
making, even if most of the time it just exists as a possibility, keeps
people in the game and playing a different game from "You had
your chance. It's too late now. The decision is made."

There is a footnote to add. Conditional decision making
doesn't mean that every decision can be challenged by anyone in
the organization and then retooled. When someone comes in protesting a decision, that individual can be asked whether an appeal
has been taken through appropriate channels, through the senate,
through the faculty union, or whatever. If not, he can be instructed
to follow procedures.

Conditional decision making is sometimes tough on the

members of an administrative team. All of us have some tendency
to wish our "boss" to be a tiger, susceptible only to modifications
of behavior we ourselves suggest. We can then be a friend to all
and the successful and humane pleader for reasonableness in a
brittle world. From there, however, it is easy to slide over into taking the hard line and to demand that the boss assume the job of
making our bad decisions stick.

   The Cultural Demand for a Muscle Administrator. There are
times when the president must grab the flag, run to the top of the
hill, and plant it. The ability to respond to these demands appro-
priately, and to differentiate such a legitimate summoning of the
office to symbolic occasion from cries for-"strong presidential leadership" that have a different meaning, separates the best administrators from those who fall short of the mark. The demand that
the symbolic leadership of the office be exercised shades gradually
into a demand from some constituencies of the university for a
"tough," no-nonsense president who "runs a tight ship." A wag
once remarked, "Everyone wants a tough administrator, by which
they mean someone who will pursue their pet enthusiasms ruthlessly." There is a trap here, of course. The same people who demand a "tough" president will not regard themselves as foreclosed
from criticism of the president as "unreasonable" or even "tyran-
nical" when they disagree with him or her. During the presidential
search and screen process at a southern university, for example,
the student newspaper commented on the opinion of one regent:
"Ferguson criticized USF's first president John Allen's administration as being 'Milquetoast' and the university's last permanent president Cecil Mackey's regime as 'dogmatic' " (*Oracle,* 1977).

   It is, or course, far more damaging from the muscle perspective to be a Milquetoast than to be dogmatic. In order to meet
the demands of those who want a muscle administrator in the president's office, and yet one who gets the job done, administrators
develop masking devices or facades. These facades include (1) talking hard and settling soft; (2) talking tough and then forgetting
about it; (3) charging through the organization like an elephant,
but then having people available to sweep up after the elephant;
(4) being exceedingly tough on noncritical issues, such as punctual
attendance at meetings, and reasonable on more important mat-

ters; (5) acting tough and scaring business away; (6) being a tiger outside the organization and a pussycat inside (Walker, 1976).

Finally, it should be reemphasized that the role of the president using a political democratic style can, indeed, be proactive.* The style has been described as "pushy diplomacy." The president can be symbolically high profile when such behavior is appropriate. In style and flair, his activities can resemble those of a successful prime minister of England. To this extent, therefore, it might be well to heed the counsel of Lord Salisbury, prime minister of England in the 1890s, who advised that diplomatic victories were won by "a series of microscopic advantages; a judicious suggestion here, an opportune civility there, a wise concession at one moment and a far-sighted persistence at another; of sleepless tact, immovable calmness and patience that no folly, no provocation, no blunder can shake" (Tuchman, 1966, p. 31). In an informal discussion with some members of a faculty concerning styles of presidential leadership, one faculty member commented that a president should really be a benevolent dictator. This point of view evoked disagreement, and after some discussion, one of the assembly recalled a pertinent comment of Krishnamenon to the effect that the difficulty with benevolent dictators is that they are similar to "vegetarian tigers": their habits are subject to change without notice.

When high-profile, aggressive symbolic behavior is required of the president, it is important for him or her to remember the source from which authority is derived. In democratic political organizations, authority is widely distributed. The president's job, then, is to summon that authority from its basic sources, from the people in the organization. He must remember the human and

---

*When I say administrators in the style may be extremely proactive, I do not set aside the fact that an administrator never knows how much will be the influence of his activities in the organization. To take an observation made by Lewis Thomas out of context, "We do not, in any real way, run the place. It runs itself, and we are part of the running" (*Time*, 1978, p. 85).

Administration is ancillary. That does not mean it is necessarily trivial or unimportant. How influential it becomes, it seems to me, depends on the direction in which the effort is spent, whether it is crosscurrent of the movement of the institution, up or downstream. It is influential in ways that we do not always understand and in ways that are variable.

political rights of those people, using his authority to transact the business of the university and to move it in the directions dictated by its character and the wishes of its constituents on and off the campus.

Trustees

It will take a long time to accumulate practical wisdom about the way boards of trustees actually act, even though there is a vast literature about how they should operate. There are differences between boards. An elected board has a different agenda from an appointed board. A board that chooses its own membership has a unique texturing. Some boards meet once a month, others once a year. The size of boards varies tremendously. The trustees of private universities and their colleagues in public institutions operate from somewhat different views of their responsibilities. The problem is further compounded by boards changing their conception of appropriate board responsibilities from time to time. Before the 1960s, for example, boards generally accepted as a major responsibility the interpretation and defense of the university to the public. Since then, many boards seem to feel that their function is to represent the interests of the public in the management of the university.

Yet in spite of difficulties in describing regularities in trustees' actions or in accumulating practical wisdom about boards, trustees do demonstrate organizational behavior and are subject to the common influences attendant on their relationship to campuses. These commonalities have been noted in the literature. It would be relatively profitless to spend much time recapitulating this deposited wisdom, most of which is harmless and some of which is even helpful. But I am unable to resist the urge to add some detritus to the accumulation. Perhaps the most honest and helpful way to deal with the topic is to set forth some propositions which seem empirically sound at this moment to me:

1. A good relationship between the president and the board of trustees is critically important to a campus. Obviously, in the political environment of a university it is essential to the pres-

ident. When Robert Hutchins was asked, "What single piece of advice would you give to presidents?" he is supposed to have replied, "Take a trustee to lunch." The trustees come the closest of any group within the university community to being a permanent and natural constituency of the president.

2. Trustees will be influenced, in their decision making and deliberations, by the model they entertain of the university and the people within it. Similarly, trustees will be influenced by their perception of the appropriate role of administrators. Boards operate most effectively where the president and the board share realistic conceptions of the nature of the university and have generally favorable views of the people within its walls. Similarly, trustees function best when they assume the institution is healthy; the assumption that pathology exists calls forth pathologies. It seems almost bromidic to say, but trustees must respect the institutions they serve. Condescending or critical attitudes communicate themselves quickly and subtly through the organization.

3. Trustees gradually develop a self-image that influences the tone of their transactions. The president has a role in establishing that tone, as does the chairperson of the board. Needless to say, an atmosphere of sophistication, fairness, respect for colleagues, and orderly and impartial procedures, with an absence of personal "showboating," can only help the campus. Pettiness, reprisal behavior, parochialism, and chaotic procedures can make the years go by very slowly for a president and, indeed, for a college or university.

4. The most commonly accepted piece of wisdom in the writings and discussions about the role of trustees is that trustees should fix policy and stay out of management, while presidents and other administrators should manage the institution. Some people carry this belief so far as to suggest that trustees should limit themselves to selecting the president and to reviewing the programs of the university and the performance of personnel.

At least two observations should be made concerning this point of view. First, the distinction between policy and management will never be completely resolved if the board is active and interested in the affairs of the university. What constitutes administration and what constitutes policy will be continuously negotiated by the administration and the board. And second, if trustees do take part in day-to-day administrative affairs, the result is better if they are thoroughly involved. The greatest mischief is caused by trustees moving into university problems just enough to complicate them, feeling free to retreat when the flack comes up and then moving in again just in time to recomplicate matters. Sometimes, to have an interested trustee thoroughly involved in all the ramifications of an administrative problem improves the relationships between an administration and a board. Trustees come to see that there are no easy "fixes" for campus problems and that problems are probably being reasonably well handled by hard-working and honest people. There are worse things than that.

Parenthetically, I have an impression that trustees are more tempted to dabble in day-to-day management where the institution is well run. The trustees of campuses with obvious problems see the disarray. Sensing the hazards of casual interference, they often stay at a distance for fear of causing explosions. But in institutions running smoothly, trustees sometimes develop the tantalizing feeling that all they need do is reach out and give matters a little push in order for problems to be straightened out immediately. Of course, it is never that simple.

5. Boards of trustees have tremendous power and yet are relatively less structured than other groups within the university. That arrangement can spell trouble. The best boards tend to structure their relationships with the campus and to manage their own affairs in regular and orderly ways.

6. The board should be encouraged to set time aside to examine its own procedures and distribution of effort. This is a difficult thing for boards to do. They don't often get around to really critical self-examination.

7. Except where the trustees serve as the final review board for personnel cases, trustees should leave personnel cases alone. Personnel cases are always more complicated than trustees are able to realize. They can be explosive. One of the most difficult lessons for a trustee is to learn that the truth is never pure and seldom simple. The trustee who persistently believes anything that is whispered is bad news for an institution.

8. The president should never threaten the board with his or her resignation, unless he really means it. No matter how such a specific confrontation is resolved, once a president threatens to resign, the clock is ticking. From then on, in my observation, it's just a matter of time.

9. As a matter of practical wisdom, presidents should resist the tendency to accept specific assignments and instructions from an individual member of the board. Since the president is employed by the total board, he should receive direction from all the trustees when they are in solemn conclave assembled. No president can work effectively for ten or twenty individual bosses.

10. The president owns the action of the trustees even if he or she has protested that proposed action. Sooner or later, if trouble results and goes on long enough, it's the president's problem.

11. Complete honesty, in the long term, is a matter of practical wisdom, to say nothing of ethics. It is best to be totally candid and open with the board of trustees. Items that the trustees would be interested in, or alarmed about, should be red-flagged for trustee attention. Nobody likes surprises. Attempts to hide problems, or to cosmetically disguise them, can only result in worse problems later.

12. Macho fantasies on the part of trustees create problems for a president, who is pushed into intemperate and confrontational behavior. Such fantasies are not repaired by unsatisfactory experience with the model of muscle administration.

13. Boards of trustees, too, have their ups and down. There will be good meetings and bad meetings. In the long pull, it is the average level of performance that counts. A good board of trustees is a joy forever.

Six

Solving Problems by Teamwork, Coalition, and Negotiation

I would hope that much of this book comes across as practical and useful, but in this chapter in particular I would like to offer some specific suggestions for applying the style of administration described in the preceding pages. These suggestions fall into two broad categories: problem solving and the formation of administrative teams.

The Hazards of Brittleness

I remember a story in a childhood adventure magazine in which the critical incident occurred when a mountain climbing party was scaling a precipice. An emergency arose. The party had to detour across the sheer, smooth rock face of a cliff. One member of the party simply froze in the middle of the transition. The leader of the party commented that since the climber had frozen and would not move, there was no hope for him. The imperiled man, hearing the alternative, move or die, finally managed to force himself forward until he was out of danger. I'm not enough of a mountain climber to know whether the event even approaches reality, but obviously the description stayed with me. It has seemed to me that, in less dramatic terms, the same phenomenon occurs in administration. I notice that in times of campus crisis, one or more administrators will have a tendency to freeze, to become brittle and unyielding. Hard and fast plans, unmovable strategies, unshakable ideologies are always vulnerable—"Whom the gods would destroy they first make brittle." When some member of the team freezes in position, the others often simply have to work around him or her.

Sometimes an unsophisticated administrator, believing he is paid to take a "strong" position, adopts brittleness under the illusion that he is thereby doing his job. After that, he demonstrates his strength by being a rock that the waves break over. Those breaking waves throw spray on everybody. The job of an administrator is not to be a rock but to solve problems. Brittleness, sooner or later, results in the administrator's becoming part of the problem.

Fighting the Problem. One form of brittleness is to rigidly resist the very existence of difficulties. But it does no good to protest and howl about them. It's a real world. We work with the problems that come to us. We do not choose them, although, regrettably, sometimes we are part of their creation. Fighting problems simply wastes energy; administrators should concentrate instead on reaching solutions. Someone once said that we are all judged by how skillfully we play the cards we are given, not how eloquently we complain about the deal. Yet despite the apparent truth of this principle, we occasionally have difficulty recognizing when we're violating it. "How can the faculty possibly pass a resolution like that? I won't stand for it! I'm sending a letter that blasts them in no uncertain terms." Thus begins a long love affair with foolishness.

One technique for avoiding too much resentment about problems is to develop a genuine appreciation for the fact that we don't learn anything on our good days. As a senior administrator once mildly observed to a junior colleague, "You're not paid for your good days. On your good days, anybody can do your job. You should be grateful that problems exist as long as you're not the reason they do."

The Definition of Problems. Before problems can be solved, even at the grass-roots level, they must be identified and defined in ways that make them solvable and in such fashion that people are willing to solve them. In my view, the responsibility for this task rests primarily with administration. In undertaking the job, administrators should beware of a couple of pitfalls. First, defining problems in terms of "good guys" and "bad guys" is not useful. For the most part, problems couched in such terms are simply unsolvable. Equally mischievous is defining problems in such a way that major elements are omitted. When this happens, the problem cannot be resolved realistically. This second error deserves an example. Representatives from three departments come to the dean and say, "There are only three secretaries remaining in the secretarial pool. These secretaries are already serving our three departments, and only ours. There are no other departments without secretarial assistance of some sort. So each of us wishes to withdraw one of the secretaries from the pool."

Perhaps the request is perfectly legitimate and will lead to greater efficiency. Mischief arises, however, when it becomes apparent that no provision has been made for the operation of the duplicating machines, a function normally handled by the pool. So the problem definition must include this fact. Problems cannot be defined out of existence.

The Problem-Solving Style

The democratic style calls for problem solving at the level closest to the problem with the simplest means available. Thus, problems are solved on the *de minimis* principle. For example, all department heads are not called together to solve a problem that a meeting of two department heads can handle unless others are also involved in the results of the decision. Similarly, the presence of deans is not required if department chairmen have all the necessary information and if the issue is not one that directly and significantly affects the deans and other constituent groups. You get better solutions when people are provided opportunities and means to handle their own difficulties and do not have to go through "daddy," whoever daddy may be.

So often the solutions to small problems appear simple to those high in the bureaucracy. And therefore they feel it's unnecessary to consult the people involved in order to get good answers. This is not always true, of course. I recall, on one occasion, walking across a branch campus of a university system in company with the chancellor. A groundsman stopped the chancellor and asked, "Do you have a minute?" I was struck with the immediate and courteous fashion in which the chancellor stopped his headlong march and other conversation, devoting his full and complete attention to the groundsman. It seemed that the gardener was having difficulty with the new and expensive sprinkler head that had been ordered by central headquarters. He expressed his concern, "Chancellor, are you familiar with these new sprinkler heads? Do you know they cost $67 apiece? Let me show you what happens to them after they've been in use a few months." He opened the top of a metal contrivance about the size of a halfback's fist and pointed to some insignificant vermiform appendix in the mechanism. He said, "That little bar breaks after a couple of hundred hours of use. When it breaks, there's nothing to do but replace the whole head. Now let me show you what happens with the old sprinkler heads." The gardener held up a gadget that, by comparison with the new shiny device, admittedly looked like a spare part for a model-T. "This old sprinkler head has that same little bar, but it's replaceable. When it breaks, all you have to do is buy another one for $.30. The chancellor asked a number of questions, thanked the groundsman carefully, made a note to call central headquarters, and went on his way.

This university system central office was not unusual in its failure to consult with the people who are closest to the problem—the groundskeepers in this case. Others have repeatedly remarked the frequency with which efficiency in private industry or business is defined exclusively in terms of efficiency to the company. In the absence of consultations, new "efficiencies" may impose endless extra hours of inconvenience on customers. Ultimately, of course, that can be expensive.

People involved in problems usually have within them the

capacity to achieve the best solutions. In such instances, the proper role of the administrator is an implementing and enabling one. The art of calling forth workable solutions from the people who must live with those solutions is too little practiced, or perceived as a preferred strategy, because administrative biases so frequently run in other directions. In more traditional models of administration, the proposed answers, if any, that come from lower levels in the pyramid are suspected of being too narrow and self-serving to be useful. I have not found this to be true. Narrow and self-serving answers develop most frequently as a reaction to preemptive and teutonic administrative styles.

There is tremendous wit and wisdom in a university. The job of administration is to call it forth and put it to work. Administrators are not usually picked because they're brighter than anyone else on the campus. In our fantasies, when problems arise in an organization, the administrator obliges by coming up with a clean, neat, bright solution that no one else has thought of. Everyone departs marveling. In the real world, this seldom happens. What can happen—and there is a vast body of literature documenting this statement—is that people solve their own problems when they feel their decisions really count and when appropriate structures have been developed to encourage such activity. Even difficult problems are better handled if people are encouraged to skin their own skunks.

All of this may seem obvious. Actually, it's a difficult and exacting style to apply. It's amazing how the assumptions of other styles slide in, almost unnoticed, and not always from the expected direction. An illustration may help. At one institution, an assistant professor in a sizable department came to a dean with whom he was personally friendly and said, "How can we get the president to take an interest in our department? We don't feel close to him. We don't feel that he appreciates us. He never notices us." The complaint was a common one on the campus, as it is on all campuses, large and small. The underlying assumption behind the complaint, to present a harsh cartoon, is that the university is the court of the Louis, the palace of the Bourbon Kings. The president is the gifted presence from whom "all blessings flow," in the words of the old hymn. The bald facts of the matter were that the de-

partment in question had never, within the memory of the complaining faculty member, had a social gathering of its own. Furthermore, the common campus view of the department was that
the members could not agree on the time of day. Yet the assumption being made was that the department would be happier if the
president met with them frequently. The president felt vaguely
uneasy and indicted by what was seemingly a perfectly humane
and reasonable request. He could only mutter that he wished he
had the time. Under the philosophy here presented, the president
should have spent more time stimulating the department to take
steps toward its own healing. The first step might be meetings of
senior members of the department with junior members. The job
of the president was to create a climate in which such activities were
encouraged.

Certainly, the presence of the president at countless events
on campus is symbolically important. But making such appearances is quite different from making a department "happy." The
very complaint of the faculty member had pyramidal and slightly
royalist assumptions built into it.

Royalist assumptions are also built into the tendency to give
the president assignments. "Ms. President, I wonder if you would
write a letter to the Department of Health, Education, and Welfare?" Here again the principle of solving problems at the lowest
level applies. A possible rejoinder to such a request is, "I'll be happy
to send such a letter. Will you prepare a rough draft for me, putting down exactly what you want me to say? I may make any necessary changes; otherwise, it can go as it is. After all, you have the
facts and know exactly what needs to be emphasized." Remember
that the request comes to the president not because she is the best
letter writer on campus but because it is assumed that the majesty
of the office will lend strength to the letter.

No Pet Solutions. To use another metaphor to describe the democratic political style: you don't make any one solution part of your
skin. Too frequently administrators become fixed on some pet answer to a problem, run into resistance, and then spend enormous
amounts of energy pushing for their favorite, when any one of
several alternatives would do just as well. For an administrator to
decide the single way the problem should be solved usually wastes

a lot of time and effort. Furthermore, as often as not, the solution is not that much better than available, workable, and uncontested options.

I'm not saying that administrators should not have strong feelings or that they should not propose solutions in order to begin the dialectic process. I'm saying they should not become so fond of a proposed solution that they interfere with the dialectic development of solutions.

I repeat, the purpose of the style is not to eliminate conflict, make everybody happy, and to have everyone agree. In the first place, this is not possible, and in the second place, it isn't desirable. The aim of the style is to make conflict creative and productive for the institution. The purpose of the style is to keep people involved in creative ways, to keep the controversies oriented to issues rather than personalities, to define problems in such a way that they are solvable. Specifically, the style is not being followed when an administrator gives commands designed to bring about a specific preferred solution and then spends exorbitant amounts of time punishing those who have not followed the commands or works tirelessly to ensure that commands are followed. There's a futile authoritarian flavor to such exercises.

No Symbolic Wars. One characteristic of less effective administrators, in my observation, is an addiction to symbolic wars. Wars by administrators against one or another constituency of the university to "teach people lessons" or simply to show administrative muscle are losers. I offer an illustration of the point.

At the university in question, there was a long tradition allowing the senior class to choose its own commencement speaker. On one occasion a final list was prepared and voted on by the class, but the preferred speakers were unavailable because the invitation was late. The first person able to accept was highly controversial. Some faculty members moved to boycott the commencement speaker. The movement aborted, but there were about a dozen members of the faculty who petitioned the president to be excused from commencement as a matter of personal conscience.

The administrative group divided on the issue. About half agreed that the responsibilities of a faculty member included attendance at commencement. They stated that to waive the rule would invite future abuse. Further, they argued that considerations of academic courtesy were involved. They urged that the faculty members who objected to the speaker should be given businesslike letters directing them to observe their obligations.

The view that prevailed was wiser in terms of the "symbolic war" principle. The faculty members were notified that although their attendance at commencement was a professional obligation, as a matter of personal conscience, they could, of course, be excused. The future abuse which some supposed would follow the decision did not occur. At the next commencement the requests to be excused did not exceed those of the "lenient" year. But had the administration insisted that the protesting faculty members attend commencement, I'm certain the feelings of resentment and of sympathy for the "martyrs" would have been much higher.

Symbolic wars are characteristic not only of university administrators but of others in positions of authority. I think of two restaurants. Both do a fair business. Both are good restaurants. At one establishment, the maitre d' sometimes turns people away if they do not have a reservation, even if the restaurant is two-thirds empty. Even when he does not turn people away, he "punishes" those who do not call in a reservation by giving them a poor table. The other restaurant does not even ask whether the party has a reservation if seats are available. Which restaurant do you think is gradually acquiring a larger clientele?

True, there are first-rate restaurants in large cities that do, indeed, attempt to maintain their reputation by refusing all non-reservation customers, regardless of available capacity. The pressure for their service is so great they can afford to fight symbolic wars and to "teach people lessons." They would do well under any conditions. Even though they can get away with it, in the long run this isn't the best way to treat human beings.

It's easy to forget the purpose for asking customers to make reservations. Presumably, that purpose is to provide better service to customers so that they will not have to wait and so that they will enjoy their dining experience more. When that purpose is forgotten, lesser purposes take over: to teach people to understand how good the restaurant is and to teach them not to be naughty. Universities often pay a higher price than restaurants for their mistakes.

Goals Versus Ego

Under more traditional administrative models, it is very difficult to persuade people to sacrifice ego for results. My first real lesson in such an exercise came from the governor of a state. He was a capable governor who brought great stature to the office. One day, after a shirt-sleeved conversation in his office about a proposal for which I sought support, he agreed to help. He pointed out, however, that he would be in a difficult political position. I asked him what I should do to assist him. He said, "Go home and keep quiet." I did just that. A few days later, I was astonished to see the governor quoted in the press as absolutely opposed to what I thought had been agreed upon. I went steaming back to his office and protested. He inquired mildly, "What did I tell you to do?" I answered, "Go home and shut up." He said, "When I think we ought to change that strategy, I will let you know." In the course of the next three or four weeks, criticisms of the governor's stated position began to pour in. Finally, he threw up his hands and said, "Let the will of the people be done," and publicly embraced the position on which we had agreed. Later, in discussing events, I asked him whether the technique was not too Machiavellian. He denied that his motivation was cynical, remarking, "The trick is to get support. Sometimes people have to learn what they are for by deciding what they are against."

It still struck me as too Machiavellian, but it was a good lesson for me in ego-suppression. Academics are frequently poor politicians because their egos are too bulky. They are unwilling to sacrifice immediate victory, or the appearance of victory, for long-term objectives and goals.

Problem People

When I am interviewing a prospective member of an administrative team and his first question is "What is my authority?" in my gut I know there is going to be trouble. Such a person is usually uncomfortable with grass-roots problem solving. It's a bit difficult to understand why this should be so. Most of the textbooks on administration counsel that lines of authority should be made very clear. It is my feeling, however, that most problems are not as clear as the textbooks make them sound. It's not that the question about authority is really a bad one—it just doesn't feel relevant. It implies that problems are somehow solved by the exercise of muscle. If someone knows clearly how heavy a hammer he carries, from then on it is a matter of seeing other people as nails, to use a colleague's nice metaphor. That kind of strategy, in my experience, leaves problems bouncing around the institution until they wind up in the president's office.

Another thing I look for in a prospective administrator is positive leadership skills. There is truly a great distinction between positive and negative leadership. I've known many people who could launch a campaign *against* something with a great deal of adrenaline and ability. Sometimes they are successful and they equate such success with "leadership" skills. I agree that there are real skills in leading from the barricades, but they do not necessarily correlate highly with the skills necessary to push a program through in an academic community, skills essential for an administrator. Other skills are necessary for the health of a political community but they are not sufficient.

The Use of Teams

Team styles are remarkably adapted to democratic political administration, perhaps essential to it. The use of teams in administration is not new, of course. Their value has been argued and demonstrated repeatedly. The statement of Argyris (1966, p. 18) is typical. "Why operate in groups? Indeed, some executives condemn group meetings and encourage individuals to make decisions. The only trouble with that solution is that it doesn't square with reality. Information technology has made it possible for an organization to make its goals more explicit and subject them to much more systematic analysis." The use of administrative teams and the staffing of decisions creates a climate in which problem-solving attitudes can be encouraged. The principle of "the more, the more" operates. The more a team is used, the more effective it becomes.

One of the essential roles of an administrator, in developing team styles, is to stimulate the problem-solving process. Frequent use of such phrases as "We are physicians to one another" or "Let's get the volleyball game going" will help to create a spirit of team problem solving and mutual assistance. The administrator should bear in mind, however, that this spirit of mutual aid and mutually helpful criticism takes time to develop.

Interpreting the meaning of the style and highlighting in discussions what is occurring are important. The administrator in charge of the team is also obliged to sense when workable solutions are emerging and to announce closure. But the existence of the team emphatically does not free the administrator from final responsibility for decisions. The president, dean, or whoever is chairing the meeting can sometimes clear the air by announcing, "I need your help in arriving at a wise decision, but I will take final responsibility for it." After some discussion, he may say, "It appears to me that we've moved as close together as we can. I am ready to call the shot. Now is your last chance. Not to make a decision is not a choice. We're going to go with the solution I've just heard summarized unless someone has a better idea."

Bringing in Your Own Team. Every major administrator, whether president or dean, faces the question whether to work with the team that another person has built or to bring in his own group. James March guesses that it probably doesn't make much difference. The intervening variable is time. My experience is the same as that of March. If a president brings in a new group of his "own" people, in about three or four years he will have a team. If he works with the people already in place, in about the same length of time a team will have developed.

It probably does help, however, to have at least one other person who understands the style of a particular administrator on the other side of the net to get a "ping-pong game" going. When such a person works enthusiastically at the style and with the philosophy of a newly arrived administrator, others join in more quickly. By the time there are three people in the act, the style is on its way.

An example of how someone on the other side of the net helps to start the play comes to mind. The events took place at a small college with a faculty proud of its reputation for individualism and even idiosyncrasy. The administrative staff also consisted of highly able, individualistic people. There was practically no team play. No one was consciously working to make any other member of the administrative group uncomfortable. It was just that each person had a private agenda.

A new man joined the administrative group. Sensing the situation, he made common cause with one of the able and temporarily more frustrated members of the administrative contingent already at the institution. Since it was difficult to get decisions made, the two deans made an agreement, "You help me and I'll help you. Whenever you can conscientiously do so, boost my programs and I will return the favor." This agreement gave them an enormous advantage. The volleyball game was started, with each one feeding shots to the other. Then things began to happen. Another senior member of the group, watching the play, approached the embryonic team and asked, "How do I get in the game?" They explained that nothing more subterranean was in operation than being mutually helpful when aid could be sincerely and honestly given. He signed on. Within a year, a pretty good team was in operation.

Physicians to One Another. In a team, it's nice if the members have good relationships with one another. Even when they do not, proper perceptions of the role of the team as problem solver can yield a good result. In my experience, the quality of the interactions among the members of the team goes up and down. Sometimes they are good and sometimes bad. It helps relations if the leader of the team interprets favorably the motives and actions of members to one another. Sometimes, this practice is difficult to remember and follow, since the leader of the team probably experiences as much frustration when things go wrong as any other member. But if an attitude can be cultivated that the members of the team are physicians to one another, the perception can be very healing. No one is strong in every area.

A perceptive colleague once pointed out a fringe benefit of the team style: it is the only style that really effectively trains administrators. More traditional approaches to administration turn the executive cadre into a mixed batch of performers and observers. If the members of a team can accept the view that each participant helps compensate for the weaknesses of the others, the results can be surprisingly worthwhile. The philosophy of mutual aid can include open, honest, and sometimes harsh, criticism if such activities are perceived as a part of the style. It takes work.

In discussing team styles, I should emphasize that the members of a team do not actively assist one another all the time. Team spirit will be most apparent in crisis, or in some endeavor requiring focused effort, such as a budget presentation.

Credit Sharing. John F. Kennedy used to say with some cynicism, "Victory has a hundred fathers. Defeat is an orphan." However, this is actually a counsel of hope, not of despair. Let everyone own the victory. If people feel they have had a hand in a good result, future solutions have a much better chance of success. I am increasingly convinced that credit is a commodity that can be widely shared without appreciably diminishing the individual portion. It is even possible for an atmosphere to be developed in which people are at some pains to pass credit around. The old game of "king of the mountain," to see who can stay on top of the credit pile, tends to be abandoned under a democratic political style.

Rounding Up "Nice Guys" for the Team. In a discussion of the democratic political style with a group of seasoned presidents, one inquired, "Where do you find a whole team of low-key, problem-solving 'nice guys' to carry on the style?" The question reflects a misunderstanding. The style can operate with a variety of personalities and accommodate all kinds of behavior on the part of administrators, including teutonic behavior on occasion. Sometimes in the chemistry of the situation, a "hard-line" administrator or two provides a kind of a dialectic inside the team and reemphasizes the problem-solving strategy and its dominance in the style. Again, let me emphasize that the style depends not on the personality characteristics of team members but on perceiving the administrative enterprise as a democratic and political process operating in an institution with a metabolism of its own. That does not mean, of course, that some personality types are not going to be more comfortable in the style than others.

The Little Red Hen Complex. One pathology of team styles is a disorder in decision making. Let's call it the Little Red Hen complex. Recent generations may not have been exposed to the fable of the little red hen who decided to bake bread. "Who will help me plant the wheat?" she asked. No one was willing to help. The little red hen planted the wheat herself. "Who will help me cultivate the wheat?" the little red hen asked of each animal in the barnyard. Again, there were no volunteers. The little drama was played out through several pages, with invitations being extended to help gather the grain, to grind the grain, to bake the grain. All the farmyard animals were indifferent to the process until the little red hen asked, "Who will help me eat my bread?" All of the animals enthusiastically volunteered. Then, that snotty little red hen ate all the bread herself. And why not? Wasn't her action a justified reward for her own effort, and also a thoroughly deserved punishment for the goof-offs?

I have news. The little red hen is alive and well and living among us. There are many num-num jobs in a university that involve extraordinarily hard and boring effort. Perhaps this applies to every position some of the time. The individuals performing such tasks can easily drift into thinking that "since I have done all the work, I will make all the decisions." There is a certain rough justice in this point of view. The problem is that most decisions from people in positions of responsibility affect other people. I personally do not subscribe to the view that registrars, librarians, and financial aid officers are the most susceptible to the little red hen complex, but their actions are noticed more frequently and more quickly than those of less visible hens. Who wouldn't notice an admissions officer who began to embezzle away institutional policy by his day-to-day admissions decisions? Who would not be aware of the librarian operating with the view that his real assignment was to protect all the books from those sloppy, indifferent potentially larcenous book molesters who carry volumes off or misfile them outrageously when left to wander through the shelves?

It is not a perfect world. But at least democratic administrative styles do help to pull everyone into the decision-making process and to give those most involved an influential role, although not a monopoly. Under more traditional models, too often the little red hen types get done in by administrators somewhere up the line who become highly annoyed and take all meaningful decision making out of the hands of those they regard as little red hens. That isn't fair either, and it doesn't work well.

Committees. When this subject comes up, aphorisms abound.

"For God so loved the world that He did not send a committee."

"If you can't commit yourself, committee yourself."

"A committee is a group created by the unable to get the unwilling to do the unnecessary."

Anyone who has worked in organizations for any period of time can add to this list of snide aphorisms. Some of the criticism of committees, of course, is more sober and more serious. "There is no sense in substituting the machinery of democracy for its spirit. Yet that is what a great deal of committee government really amounts to. Such waste of scholarly time and effort can be avoided with no loss to genuine democracy, which is a spirit of government, not a mechanism" (Wriston, 1959, p. 121). Sometimes the criticism is less cerebral. "The second way for avoiding decisions, or seeming to do so, is used on issues on which the teacher-professor set is likely to be especially excited. The system probably was invented in schools, but it has spread like locusts in a bad year. It consists of committees. Their appeal to the naive mind is tremendous. Committees appear to turn underlings into administrators who thus feel the importance of their votes on everything" (Marshall, 1977, p. 11).

Nicholas Murray Butler, president of Columbia University about the time of World War I, seemed somewhat accepting of the committee system, but separated the execution of policy from the development of policy. He said: "Fussy administration manifests itself chiefly through the committee system which is a plural executive with necessarily divided responsibility. Many minds chosen for their representative character and capacity are needed to formulate and to settle questions of policy, but when policies are once formulated and settled, they are far better executed by a single individual than by a number of men acting in consultation" (Knight, 1940, pp. 112–113).

Part of the hostile attitude toward committees goes back to the historic emphasis on individualism in our society. This culture has a long tradition of celebrating the contributions of individual genius rather than the achievements of groups. After all, Ne vton did not make his observations on gravity after consulting with a committee of his knowledgeable colleagues (although who is to say how much he owed to discussions with his peers?). Edison did not invent the electric light because of the dazzling insight of a committee of fellow workers. Kant did not write the *Critique of Pure Reason* nor did Leonardo paint the Mona Lisa as a result of skillful exercises in consensus building.

Still, it's obvious that even these giants "stood on the shoulders of giants." The Mona Lisa, after all, does not resemble the painting of a geisha by a Japanese artist. It is a product of an artist and a culture. The phenomenon of simultaneous invention also illustrates the principle.

Since, however, the ambivalence to committees runs deep in the society, administrators are usually apologetic about using them, even though they are and must be frequently used in complex organizations. I believe committees are undeserving of their poor reputation. In addition to cultural biases, their generally unflattering reputation derives from the fact that so few people possess the skills necessary to work effectively with colleagues. Those skills have not been sufficiently identified or attended to. Every experienced administrator knows that people have different levels of ability to work with committees and get satisfactory results.

A number of observations seem useful.

1. The climate of expectation influences the effectiveness of committees. Climate is a subtle set of attitudes created over a period of time. I have noticed that when committee effectiveness begins to improve, similar improvement seems to occur everywhere at about the same time throughout an institution.

2. Committee members should be selected on a functional basis. They should include people who have technical expertise as well as representatives of those groups that will be affected by the decision. The problems addressed must be important to committee members.

3. The leadership of committees is important. If individuals are available on the top team who have skills at working with committees, they can be invaluable. Too frequently top administration tends to move away from leadership positions in committees.

The symbolic role of the leader is important. As noted, the president of an institution can achieve satisfactory results from a committee where others have failed: this, not because of superior skill or training but because of the authority of the office.

4. It helps to develop sensitivity to the predictable psychol-

ogy of committees. There is nothing written, of which I am aware, to guide the administrator in these areas. I have observed that certain kinds of events in committees can be anticipated. The "show stopper" is an example. The committee has a difficult and controversial assignment. Things seem to be moving through the committee very laboriously, but generally progressing. An influential member of the committee has said very little, but has been fairly effective, although unenthusiastic. After two or three meetings of the group and toward the end of a long session, the individual in question, usually an opinion leader in the academic community, blows up. "That does it! I have gone as far as I can with this complete and utter nonsense. I have *tried* to be flexible. Believe me, I have. You will never know how hard I have tried. I have compromised away everything except my basic principles. Now I am at the end of the line. I can't go along with anything this committee has decided." This is usually the time that committees dissolve, after the chairperson figuratively throws up and faints. Yet the scenario just presented is more the rule than the exception when divided committees have to deal with emotional issues. When assignments are difficult and feelings are deeply split, people give up too soon.

The technique is to accept such detours as normal and to go back and start over again. "All right, Fred isn't able to go along with us. Perhaps we have been moving too fast. Let's go back to square one and start again." Of course, there will be groans. There may even be a resignation or two from the committee, although such events are rarer than one might think from the stereotype. A skillful leader can then work around the holdout until the committee has worked well down the road again past the position veto of the protester. At this point an invitation to the holdout to examine his or her motivation, and to decide whether he really wants the problem solved or not, sometimes works.

There are other techniques. I should interject here that early in the game the committee members should be polled about their willingness to solve the problem. It seems a little stagy, but when everyone has pledged allegiance to seeking a solution, and a realistic one, it influences the chemistry of the committee in beneficial ways.

5. Nothing I have said should be interpreted to mean that dissident opinion in a committee is undesirable. It is essential for

the dialectic to operate. Opposing views strengthen the final report of the committee and serve to safeguard against hasty or ill-advised actions. Blocking behavior is not to be confused with legitimate and necessary dissent.

6. Too frequently, committees work in isolation. Committee members should consult with others who will be affected by their decisions. Sometimes committees can develop an artificial sense of sovereignty. They may succumb to the tendency to make unilateral recommendations based on inadequate consultation and then to take the position: "The job was assigned to the committee. We have done our work. Now it's up to the administration to do with the report what they will. There is nothing else to discuss." Such an attitude shows that committees too must be sensitized to their role as problem solvers rather than law givers. A problem-solving orientation can be created in groups, as well as in individuals. When committees develop this orientation, they won't quit until a satisfactory solution is achieved. In this connection, if things do go wrong after a report is issued, the committee may have to be reconvened to examine fresh data or to receive reports from constituent groups that may have been missed. With the right point of view, committees time and again perform in truly heroic fashion.

7. It is important to decide before going into a committee meeting, or even calling the meeting, what you hope to achieve from such a gathering. That does not mean such expectations should operate as a secret iron agenda in back of all the discussion. They merely provide a sense of direction. South of that point, being flexible and alert, being willing to compromise and to accept alternate solutions are essential.

Resistance and Inertia. One of the benefits of the team style and of cooperative problem-solving techniques is that it becomes unacceptable for a member of the team to say, "That problem is in my area. I will get to it when I have time. In the meanwhile, everyone leave it alone because it falls in my jurisdiction."

Certainly we all need our own areas in which to work and to achieve. That need can be honored in team styles. When, however, an individual member of the team is badly stacked up, he or she should be encouraged to call on less pressured colleagues for assistance. When he does not, the problem can be given to a team or simply assigned to someone else. The point has to be made repeatedly: "Not solving the problem is not an acceptable alternative." The democratic, problem-solving style is not created to defend either egos or structure, but to get the job done.

Of course, certain resistances do develop to the style I am discussing. Critics of team styles point to the exorbitant amount of time they require. I have a suspicion that if the visible time required in team effort were balanced against the invisible time spent in overturning individually taken decisions, the balance might be pretty even, a point made more than once in this book.

Finally, bear in mind that an administrator need not be a prisoner of committee action. Even this statement, though, sets up a false dichotomy between a team leader and a team. Problems are to be worked through. The spirit of cooperative problem solving is the goal to be achieved. All the suspected pathologies that have been attributed to the committee system are the result, for the most part, of inadequate leadership skills and unperceptive readings of the subtleties and nuances of committee behavior.

Seven

Moving Beyond
a Human Relations
Approach

Can the political style be distinguished from the human relations
approach to administration? Yes. A political style does not have the
same emphases as administrative styles that are rationalized by human relations research. I am not trying to suggest that politically
effective administrators and human relations administrators are
totally different breeds distributed bimodally in attitudes and perceptions, if not behavior. I am merely pointing out that there seems
to be a subtle difference in focus. Effective political administrators
concentrate on institutional climates and structures more than on
individuals as such, although the human relations concern is surely
there. In the political style, people need not change their characters
or personalities for the style to succeed. It is more a matter of
changing the way they see the university operating. To put it another way, the political style tries to make the institution better

153

rather than to persuade people to be better. The best administrators stress the building of structures and the creation of perceptions that help people with very different kinds of toilet training
interact effectively. Certainly people with quite varying personalities can work together to conduct a good commencement exercise,
for example. In fact, people who individually may be quite disor-
dered can interact successfully under the proper conditions. And
conversely, people who are entirely healthy from a psychological
point of view may be involved in very pathological organizational
relationships.

Although the political and human relations approaches differ in some respects, then, they are similar in requiring certain
attitudes or abilities that might be characterized as human relations
skills. Among these are trust, the willingness to forgo reprisal, and
knowing how to time certain actions.

Trust

Trust is a prerequisite to the effectiveness of any administrative style or the creation of effective institutional climates. William James once remarked (1897, p. 24), "A social organism of any
sort whatever, large or small, is what it is because each member
proceeds to his own duty with a trust that the other members will
simultaneously do theirs. A government, an army, a commercial
system, a ship, a college, an athletic team, all exist on this condition
without which, not only is nothing achieved, but nothing is even
attempted." Rufus Miles (1969, p. 355), while a lecturer at the
Woodrow Wilson School of Public and International Affairs at
Princeton University, made a similar observation: "The element of
human behavior which is central to an analysis of organizations
under stress is that of mutual trust. It is the cement which holds
the organization together. It is the mortar between its human
bricks. Where trust is high, an organization can stand an unbelievable amount of buffeting; where it is low, a seemingly innoc-
uous incident may set off a chain reaction of crumbling human
relationships." Trust is fundamental to effective administration.
The perceptions and structures of the democratic political style
of administration foster trust.

Trust cannot be commanded or coerced. It is a reasonable

hypothesis that people learn to trust by first being trusted. Unfortunately, university administrators who obviously and easily trust faculty members and students are not as plentiful as one might believe from the rhetoric.* And therefore the distrust expressed or implied by the majority of administrators—as well as by other leaders toward their constituents—is reciprocated.

This general temper and mood of distrust makes the style I am talking about seem to go against the tide of "common sense." Speaking of this mood in relation to politics, Joan Cook (1975, p. 12) comments: "In the political sphere, there is a growing suspicion between the governed and the governors. The people suspect that their political leaders are selfish and untrustworthy; and the leaders in turn treat the people with contempt and condescension, encouraging them to be obedient and silent." In the same spirit, John Gardner observes ruefully, "The foes of freedom are still ready to argue that the unruliness, sloth, and the savage self-indulgence of men make a free society simply impractical. The world is full of people who believe that men need masters" (1961, p. 147).

And so we have a predicament. Trust is low in the society and yet is essential to any kind of successful leadership, including administrative leadership. The editors of *Time* ("In Quest of Leadership," July 15, 1974, p. 35), in a long and searching essay on the subject, offered the following advice: "To make leadership possible, the essential link between leaders and followers must be restored: trust. As Toynbee has put it, the leader must 'make his fellows his followers.' This can happen only if they trust him enough not to examine or attack each of his individual actions and are willing to go along with him for a while."

In summary then, while trust is necessary for any organization to function at its best, there is a general mood of distrust in

---

*I have talked with a number of presidents and administrators who are willing to concede that a great deal of decision-making authority must be left with faculty and students in many areas, but who frequently add a footnote such as, "But there is one area in which faculty cannot be trusted with that kind of responsibility and that is budgeting." Or, "There is one place where you really can't depend on faculty to make honest and wise decisions and that's promotion." Interestingly, not all of the presidents have the same list. What one president will trust the faculty to do, another will not.

the society that makes the problem of establishing such trust difficult and demanding. It is my view that the democratic political style provides a climate that is more hospitable to the development of trust than styles built on more traditional hierarchical assumptions. Finally, I believe it is the responsibility of administrators to take the initiative. What it means to trust is not always as obvious as it might seem. There are some derivative propositions for administrators from the view just expressed that will make this point clearer, for example the dictum that "You can't save people from themselves."

The Freedom to Make Mistakes. Part of trusting others is giving them the freedom to make mistakes. Indeed, trying with rules and strategies to prevent them from doing so, to save them from themselves, seldom works, at least in democratic societies. Prohibition was a failure. The fact that the Ralph Nader campaign for seatbelts drifted from education to coercion probably accounted for the relative failure of the effort to get passengers in automobiles to take precautions for their own safety. The laws prohibiting the use of marijuana are not faring well. And people continue to smoke cigarettes, in spite of dire health warnings on the package.

How does all this apply to day-to-day administration? I offer an illustration. During a congested registration period, a dean decides to limit psychology sections to twenty students. Some of the psychology instructors reply to a directive on the matter: "I am really quite comfortable with thirty-five students. I'll be happy to accommodate more students in my sections." The dean responds that larger sections will result in "an inferior quality of instruction." The administrative problem is that the dean is attempting to save the professor and students from themselves. The students want in; the professors want them in. But the dean knows best. The dean is now in the role of moral philosopher, and perhaps policeman. An appeal is made to the dean of the faculty, who supports his administrative colleague. So now two administrators are involved in the game. The message that comes across to the rest of the campus is that the administration "doesn't trust people."

In the ear of my mind, I hear a colleague at this point saying, "I agree with your general message that trust is essential and that it begins on a campus with administrators trusting others. I certainly agree that in building a climate of trust, it's first necessary to eliminate, or at least minimize, administrative actions based on distrust. But beyond that, I have two questions. 'Are you saying the dean has no business worrying about class size?' and second, 'If you agree that the dean might have a legitimate concern, how could the problem have been addressed more creatively?' " Yes, the dean has a right to be concerned. But the first determination to be made is: Does the problem exist? If it does, I assume that others are aware of the problem and are affected by it in addition to the dean. If that is true, they should be involved in defining the problem and in the solution. If the dean is the only one who perceives a difficulty to exist, then her first job is to educate the people affected by the situation or else an attempt to change matters would be useless. Assuming that others do sense a problem, then the dean might have begun with a discussion involving affected students and faculty. Probably she would find feeling unevenly distributed concerning the matter. Some students and faculty members would be comfortable in large classes. Others would do better in small sections. The situation might be addressed by offering a combination of large and small sections with a choice for both students and faculty members.

As a rule, efforts to save us from ourselves fail because we are irritated by someone assuming they know what's best for us and thus are taking the decision out of our hands. Rather than trying to persuade people to do what is sensible and right and prudent and healthy, administrators should tackle the more realistic task: to create social climates and structures in which people are able to perform "better." The democratic political style—with its emphasis on openness, team effort, problem solving by those most affected by those problems, and orderly, agreed-upon procedures—provides a hospitable environment for the development of such organizational climates.

Avoiding Motivational Analysis. People's motives must be accepted at face value. The problem with operating on the basis of motivational analysis is that too frequently other people's motives are seen as self-serving, Machiavellian, and expedient. When the actions of others are seen in this way, the human tendency is to respond with expedient and Machiavellian countermaneuvers. Everyone becomes locked in a circle of suspicion and hostility that has its own built-in tactics and structure.

Much of the paranoia on a university campus is based on the imputation of motives. The phrase "I know what they're trying to get away with" is frequently the beginning of suspicion, profitless maneuvering, and the diminution of trust. Even were we all full-time, fully certified psychologists, psychiatrists, and psychoanalysts, we could not deal with people's motives or get inside their skins sufficiently to make motivational analysis the basis of administrative action. However, the analysis of motives fails not only because we do not know enough but because the unflattering analysis of others' motives is always one-sided. No one is a willing scoundrel. Most of us see ourselves most of the time as exemplary in motive and purpose. Isn't it the more sane course then to assume others to be as we are?

If motivational analysis is ruled out in formulating administrative strategy, the alternative is to accept people, and their actions, on their own terms. If actions and declarations are taken at face value, if favorable motivation is imputed to everyone, a positive ambience is created. All that is lacking is an appropriate structure through which people's honorable and fair motivation can be expressed. Here are a couple of examples illustrating how the structures created under a democratic political model can help avoid the pitfalls of the motivational analysis approach.

The setting is a large urban university. After considerable skirmishing and debate, a committee on faculty ethics is appointed as a standing committee of the university. There is distrust concerning motives on both sides; although the initial thrust for its establishment has come from a group of the faculty, there is considerable faculty suspicion that the committee may simply become a tool of the administration. The fear is that the committee may be used to "control" and restrict the personal behavior of faculty members. Consequently, a highly abrasive, combat-oriented, but brilliant member of the faculty is elected to chair the committee. Now it is the administrators' turn to be suspicious. Most members of the administrative group believe the new chairperson can be counted on to defend even outrageous faculty behavior. They assume he will give the administration a "hot foot" on the first cases that come before the committee. On the basis of such suspicions, fellow administrators urge the president to veto the committee's actions and to insist that another chairperson be selected. The president refuses and insists that the agreed-upon procedures be followed. She points out that she has imposed no restriction on the committee in the selection of a chairperson.

The newly elected chairperson, however, begins to study deeply the issues of professional standards and behavior. Daily conversations with administrators, as well as fellow faculty members and sometimes students, bring about a change in the posture of the chairman. He adopts a more intolerant view of faculty conduct. In fact, he begins to criticize some of the more vulnerable behavior of colleagues savagely and intemperately. The faculty is dismayed. As time passes, his activities become increasingly judgmental and punitive; he even bullies other members of the committee, who occasionally refer to him as Torquemada. The committee members seek audience with the president, pleading, "Save us from this madman!" The president replies, "You elected him. Certainly the things he is doing are not all bad. If you feel he is being unprofessional, however, there are procedures available for recall." The faculty members protest, "The so and so would never forgive us. He would be out to get us at the first opportunity. We can't do that." The president replies, "Very well, then, see the chaplain. I will not set aside the procedures agreed upon with the academic senate. I suppose you will just have to endure until the next election."

At the next election, an academic heavyweight, a veritable sumo wrestler, is elected to the position. No more solid, solution-oriented, fair, or dispassionate individual could have been chosen. Under the surface of the exchange is the insistence of the president that established procedures, and the ideology undergirding those procedures, be observed. The substitute strategy of presidential intervention because a "bad" person must be controlled is rejected.

Another example. It was promotion time. A department with a reputation for "maneuvering" submitted to the appropriate committees and administrators a list of nominees for promotion. The member of the department that people had supposed was the "star" and clearly deserving of promotion was placed last on the list. "Aha," the mind readers suggested, "the department is putting a man who clearly deserves promotion at the bottom of the list so that when he is promoted, as he must be, everyone else will be swept along or else endless grievances will be filed." As it turned out, after much soul-searching and debate, the universitywide committee recommended promotion from the top of the list, as it had with other departments in a tight budget year. When the "star" faculty member at the bottom of the department list was therefore not promoted, Macedonian howls were heard from the department. It took a long time to sort matters out. The following year, however, the process was astonishingly responsible. The "star" passed over the previous year headed the list.

Of course, matters do not always work out so happily, but the alternatives to a strict adherence to fair procedures are unsatisfactory. An institution can very gradually become a great tangled morass of motive guessing, jockeying, and attempts to outmaneuver individuals and groups if administrators act on the basis of suspicions about motives rather than adhering to established democratic procedures.

Taking People Where They Are. As I said earlier, it is relatively profitless to spend time trying to get people to be "better" or trying to head off their anticipated bad behavior. An advantage of the democratic political style is that the emphasis is elsewhere. In a sense, the basic character of people is irrelevant when this style is being used. People are not presumed to be either naturally good or naturally bad. Administration is simply not approached in this way. The best administrators of my acquaintance seem to accept people as they are and to work from that point. In their view, everyone starts with a full deck, and for the most part the potential for constructive activity outweighs the potential for mischief. In other words, they trust people's basic intention and capacity to act beneficently.

Several implications derive from this point of view. When one accepts the principle of taking people where they are, the question of "who is responsible" becomes unimportant. The relevant question when something goes wrong is rather "How did we miss it?" or "How can we improve our performance and solve the problem?" When this outlook is adhered to over a period of time, a kind of nonpersonal nonblaming approach to problems develops. Members of work teams accept and recognize their limitations as well as their strengths. Not uncommonly, after a time, someone says, "That kind of a problem is not one that I'm particularly effective in solving. Why don't we use Joe's talents? He's good at . . . ." Or again, "I may have been partly responsible for the foulup. Let's look at what we did wrong, including me." People do not hesitate to own part of a problem if personal judgments of blame are not being used as weapons.

At this juncture, it is well to emphasize a point made elsewhere. Experienced administrators, on reading these observations, may object, "But people don't always do right. Sometimes a president or a dean has to step in to prevent total disaster."

Yes, sometimes. But let us not forget the homeostatic principle involved: The more administrative intervention occurs, the more it will be required. Without shunning intervention strategies entirely, I must stress that such strategies must have a low priority on the master agenda that informs administrative efforts. If the dominant assumption being pushed and worked with is that bad people are at the heart of every problem and that they cannot be trusted, it then becomes important to prevent them from hurting themselves and others. Played out, that assumption can become the total game.

Thus, the most effective administrators I know seem to perceive institutional problems as basically suprapersonal or impersonal. People are accepted as they are, just as the materials of the carpenter, in the following example, are respected and accepted.

I have been watching the construction of a new building from the window of my office. I have noticed the way the carpenters deal with problems of construction. They don't fight the problem or the material. For instance, one carpenter was trying to pull a stubborn nail from a two-by-four with his hammer. The nail wouldn't come loose. He tried a little harder. The nail still resisted. The imp of the perverse squatted on my shoulder and I thought, "Aha, it's good to see someone who works with a hammer and nails every day have the same problems that I do when I try to build something. He won't get the nail out. He'll become frustrated. He'll wind up breaking his hammer or spraining his back trying to get the nail out."

He didn't. He simply gave up the effort and looked around

for another way to solve the problem. First he picked up a two-by-four and placed it under the hammer head to give it better leverage. The nail stayed in place. The carpenter gave up the hammer, hunted around for a crowbar, and finally eased the nail out. A short time later, the same man prepared to lift a heavy panel into place for nailing. He hefted the material and found it awkward to lift. He stopped and signaled to a colleague for help. Together, they lifted the panel and nailed it into place.

By analogy, administrators should be so smart. We should trust and accept the people and problems we work with enough to develop an attitude at least comparable to that of a carpenter toward his material. The material of the carpenter is not there to frustrate him. It is just "behaving" in a normal fashion. So, too, a university faculty, staff, and student body were not put in place to frustrate administrators. They are behaving predictably and "normally," even when they seem to be the source of problems.

We can also learn something about problem solving from these carpenters. If exerting reasonable effort on a problem does not yield a desired result, then we should back off and try something else. The democratic political style under discussion predisposes to this kind of good sense. The emphasis on alternative goals and strategies, together with the avoidance of symbolic struggles is productive. It is related to a kind of basic trust in the entire academic enterprise and the people associated with it. If one thing won't work, something else will. Such an approach goes back to the assumption of health, rather than pathology, in the organization. One of the problems with the muscle administration perspective is that it sets us up for the administrative equivalents of the broken hammer, the strained back, the red face, and the grunt. Too often, these seem like a reasonable price to pay for a "strong" managerial solution to administrative problems.

No Reprisals

I have talked about criticism and its role in relation to the democratic political view of a campus. Here I'd like to approach the same topic from a human relations perspective. If this seems repetitious, take it as a sign of importance of the topic. The most consistently identifiable contrast between the champ and the bush-leaguer in administration is the difference in their attitude concerning revenge. It serves us well to remember what Woody Allen once said, "You can never get even with the world. It takes too long and too many lawyers."

One of the occupational hazards of administration is resentment, as I pointed out in an earlier chapter. Nobody likes to be a bedpan. Still, we must accept that it is an imperfect world and human beings need other human beings to blame for difficulties. The mischief arises among administrators when a kind of Siciliano mentality develops. Of course, the urge to want to hand it back to people who hand it to you is understandable. The impulse is not always easy to detect in ourselves. But the best university administrators I know are able to manage their resentments and to avoid tendencies to get even or to "teach 'em a lesson."

This principle applies outside university administration, as well. For instance, work done at the Institute for Social Research in the University of Michigan revealed that "supervisors of high-producing groups seem in the workers' view to behave differently than supervisors of low-producing groups; they seemed to be different kinds of people. In many cases the high-producing supervisor was less punitive toward his subordinates, he supervised in general ways rather than closely, he was more likely to be concerned about his subordinates as human beings, as individuals, rather than as means for turning out a product" (Perrow, 1970, pp. 6-7).

In my observation, tournament-level administrators are nonpunitive not because they have nice-guy personalities but because they do not perceive frustrating situations as threatening. They recognize that frustration, opposition, and criticism are part of the system, expected and acceptable. In the university seen as a political system, these elements are inevitable if the system is to operate.

A final thought. Once a nonpunitive cosmology is accepted by administrators, the view must be presented continuously to the wider academic community. The presentation must be in the form of example *and* rhetoric.

Reprisal State of Mind. A newspaper columnist, in some candid observations about Henry Kissinger, remarked of him: "He was also a victim of the presidential affinity for revenge and sus-picion, a dangerous, unhealthy virus which contaminated the am-bience of the executive branch" (W. Scott, 1974). If the virus is unhealthy for the nation, it is no less virulently mischievous for a campus. Suspicions and hostility, on the part of either administra-tors or faculty members, evoke reactions and stereotypes. It is a poison. It is the job of administrators not to punish the wicked but to solve problems. Many administrative teams include individ-uals who, for the best of motives in their own eyes, succumb to the "correctional" view of the administrative role. Not infrequently, such an individual will acquire some nickname, such as "the Car-dinal." A person like this has a keen sense of moral justice and a honed sense of personal responsibility for rectifying wrongs. A typ-ical rationalization from such an administrator will be, "I am not trying to pay anyone back. I am trying to teach them a lesson. I want to show them that they can't get away with shoddy behavior like that."

Forget it! Attitudes of this sort call forth a dialectic response, since few people see themselves as wicked, and still fewer will lie still under moral condemnation. And furthermore, "the Cardinal" himself is always perceived as a sinner in his own right by someone. The game of slap and dodge can go on forever. The strategy is ineffective; but more that that, the tone imparted to the adminis-trative effort by the "sin-killer" psychology is destructive.

The reprisal state of mind is based on a cops-and-robbers view of administration. Find the "good guys," identify the "bad guys," and then punish the wicked. Most administrative problems are infinitely more complex than that. The effort to categorize people as "incompetent" and "competent" or "bad" and "good" is debilitating and largely useless. People are complex. Their strengths are also weaknesses, depending on the context in which they are applied. The style under discussion, in contrast to the more tra-ditional "muscle" perspective on administration, tends to eliminate the game of cops and robbers.

Unwilling to Be Villains. The hunt for villains fares especially poorly when all sides of a problem are examined. An example of the complexity of bad-guy hunting is illustrative. A faculty mem-ber I knew was unpopular with administrators. He was abrasive and took delight, according to reports, in spreading tales unflattering to one or another dean, department head, and often the president. His reputation was one of "lying" about his mistreatment at the hands of administrators. He was accused of being totally indifferent to the facts and obviously dedicated to causing trouble.

The faculty member came to the office of the president one day to complain that a grant request he had filed twelve weeks earlier had simply been "lying around in administrative offices" for the entire time. Now the granting agency was pushing him for a reply. The situation was, he declared, intolerable and revealed again the number of "goof offs" and "goof ups" in the administrative ranks. He proposed a slate of two or three primary scoundrels. Investigation revealed that nearly every administrator was thoroughly out of patience with this person. They too had heard the accusation that the grant proposal had been "lying around" for twelve weeks. No one, however, was consciously conspiring to frustrate the man. No one was deliberately blocking the proposal, but apparently there were ambiguities surrounding it. And no one was particularly eager to take the initiative or to exert the effort required to resolve these problems, particularly since a half-dozen administrators at different levels had already given an hour or two apiece to discussing the problems of the proposal with the faculty member. They had urged him to make some adjustments and to supply additional information on two or three points. From their perspective, the next move was up to the faculty member. They perceived him to be uncooperative and the major source of the delays.

Thus the administrators felt there were many difficulties with the proposal yet to be resolved, whereas the faculty member thought their suggestions were harassing and trivial or, indeed, just plain wrong. In his view, he had already settled these difficulties by negotiating with the sponsoring agency; end of case! The administrators objected that nothing was in writing and the university might be left holding the bag. They were unwilling to proceed on the basis of vague and unwritten understandings. Eventually, skillful questioning on the part of two or three administrators helped to repair information gaps. A little serious effort that grew out of a meeting of several people with the faculty member finally brought a solution. Not an unusual saga.

Unquestionably, there was truth on both sides. And there were resistances and injured feelings on both sides. But there were no willing villains.

Futility of Punishment. Those few administrators who seem obsessed with the need to punish perceived misbehavior on the part of faculty members or students argue that if bad conduct is not punished, people will learn they can get away with misconduct. The same argument is advanced for refusing to reverse administrative decisions as a result of "pressure."

In my observation, it never happens. People come away from problem-solving sessions that are constructive with feelings of relief and appreciation. The sneers that are sometimes directed toward administration do not come because an administrator failed to punish someone or because an administrator changed his mind as a result of argument or "pressure" from the faculty or students. To profit from punishment, people have to see a relationship between the punishment and the crime, but even more, they must be made to feel that a crime has been committed. That's a neat trick. I am not sure I have ever really seen it pulled off. I remember an account of the end of the criminal career of an old-time mobster. As he was shooting it out with the police, barricaded in an apartment, he wrote on a piece of paper spattered with his own blood, "This is what I get for defending myself." Now, if that's true of a leading public enemy, I wonder how many willing volunteers for the scoundrel role we are going to find on campuses? All administrators do when they attempt to punish is to hurt and anger people and to alienate them.

Unimportance of Saving Face. When the urge to visit reprisals is not rooted in a primitive delight in retribution, it comes from a defense of self. Traditional models of administration predispose administrators to worry too much about losing face. They become committed to actions that are manifestly unwise on the basis of the argument "If I back down now, it will be misinterpreted by the faculty," or "If I back down now, I will seem to be wrong."

I'll say it again. Administrators must concentrate on the role of problem solvers. It does not pay to be too worried about how one's actions are interpreted. If an administrator is trusted and liked, the best interpretation will usually be placed on his actions anyway. Regrettably, it works the other way also.

Sometimes when a fuss arises between campus administrators, both reluctant to back down because of "appearances," I follow a principle suggested by a seasoned college president: "It is the job of the bigger man to give in." That dictum tends to reverse the dominant cultural stereotype that the man "on top" always wins the argument and, when he meets serious resistance, uses muscle to carry the day. When the obligation to be mature and statesmanlike is taken as a responsibility of the superordinate position, it's amazing how many problems can be resolved without impasse. Of course, there are exceptions. I am talking about a prevailing strategy.

I have noticed that sometimes administrators, in talking about some type of interpersonal problem that has come up, lose sight of their objective, which is to solve a problem and achieve a particular result. Instead, they become more interested in self-vindication. Such statements as "I gave him a piece of my mind" or "I told him where to get off" usually represent a failure to keep a goal in mind that is broader and more worthwhile. The vindication of personal feelings, the demonstration of how tough one is or how courageous one can be in verbal combat, is usually an objective contradictory to such goals as changing behavior or perceptions or otherwise achieving a result that is in the best interests of the university. An administrator, regardless of style or ego needs, has fulfilled his purpose if the problem has been solved.

Providing an Honorable Path of Retreat. It is a truth of politics, not just a rule of humanity, that when we really have someone on the run, when we have the facts dead right, we have difficulty resisting the temptation to rub our opponent's nose in it. The exercise is expensive, though. Offering nonthreatening retreat is one way to lead people into the nonblaming, problem-solving psychology, as well as to avoid creating an enemy. There are always acceptable reasons why people make mistakes. They had misinformation. They did not have enough information. They had been misled. If the nail has to be driven home and the situation clearly and unequivocally pinned down, then explanations for the mistake should be made available. "I recognize that you did not have complete information on this problem. It was not easily available to you," or, "Your indignation is understandable in view of what you thought had taken place."

Timing

Being sensitive to people involves being sensitive to time and how it affects them. People are frequently "bent out of shape" not just by an action or word in itself but by the timing of that action.

When to Push. Someone has remarked that in politics timing is everything. Certainly it is most important in the political model of university operation. Some administrators, on first hearing the democratic style described, tend to think of the administrative role as more inert than it actually is. The role is active, even "pushy," as I pointed out earlier.

Thus, one of the key sensitivities an effective administrator needs to develop is an intuition concerning the proper time to push. The decision must usually be intuitive, but there are some guidelines. The answers to a number of questions can be critical. What is the attitude of significant opinion groups on the campus? Is the issue one that agitates the faculty alone or the students also? Might the issue be joined easily to other causes and thereby build emotional reactions? Does the issue predispose supporters and opponents to form coalitions? Is it symbolic? Does it deal with values fundamental to the perspectives of the students, faculty, or staff? Finally, is the administrator doing the pushing generally in good repair at this particular time? An administrator who is in good shape has more sliding room than one who is not.

These questions all presuppose resistance to action. Where a campus is ready for movement and change—no problem. When administrative action is the beginning of the dialectic calling forth opposition, then judgments are in order. Where administrative initiative will be resisted by both faculty members and students, then movement must be slow, with time for interpretation and diplomacy. And where the issues can become symbolic to the academic community, such as the introduction of a controversial program, then timing also becomes most important.

Accordion Effect. There is a pulse in the life of a campus. There are times for great effort and times when it is possible to sit back and watch. I have noticed that young administrators are occasionally lost to administration because they failed to understand that this pulse also affects the workload. Sometimes faculty members going into administrative positions are genuinely shocked by the seemingly overwhelming pressure of the work volume. They believed the stereotype that all an administrator does is answer the mail and make rather neat, even if stupid, decisions. After two or three weeks of unrelenting pressure, the tendency is to feel, "This is too much. I can't work like this for the rest of my life. I never see my family. I am beginning to get ulcers. The smartest thing to do is quit."

Such potential casualties should be told about the accordion effect in administrative work load. Certainly there are periods, and sometimes long periods, of sustained effort, but except in the most wildly overworked teams, the pressure inevitably relents, allowing periods for more leisured reflection and planning.

The problem is not so acute for administrators who use work as an anesthetic for anxiety, as many, perhaps most, tend to do from time to time. A continuing and unrelenting workload is often self-generated. Not that there isn't always work to do, but under conditions of anxiety, many administrators use busyness as a talisman. If they work hard and observe all the proper cultural values, right will magically prevail. There is a trap, however. Many times when a critical agenda is political, their too great immersion in pick-and-shovel work can divert them from the main issues being addressed behind the facades.

A more subtle aspect of timing has to do with the pacing of effort. I have noticed a tendency, particularly in inexperienced administrators, to lunge at a problem, hit it full force, then lose interest if immediate results are not obtained, and finally lunge at some other problem. In the long haul, solving administrative difficulties that are complex sometimes seems like hauling a wagon out of the mud with a team of horses. The kind of labor that gets the job done is not lunging but a slow and steady pull.

No Surprises. I no longer remember whether the observation is original with me, but one of the secrets of getting along in university administration is the same secret that helps one survive on a snake farm: Keep moving but don't make sudden jerky moves. Universities are notoriously subject to "startle" reactions. So most changes of importance to an academic community require time. A corollary of this fact is that in spite of the cries for stronger wine and madder music, moderation is usually the best policy.

Very frequently the call for instantaneous action has in it a disguised punishment agenda for someone. That the thirst for immediate action does not always come from objective and verifiable time pressures is illustrated by the way people respond when an administrator applies the formula "If you have to have an answer today, the answer is no." I have been a little surprised at how frequently time stretches out when that rule of thumb is used. On sober reflection, those who think something must be done immediately realize that perhaps there is enough time to consult and to have some questions answered.

A great deal can be accomplished if there is enough time — or lost if there isn't, as we see in the next case. The problem was a common one: faculty office space was unevenly distributed. Gradually, as new buildings were added to the campus, some departments had acquired large offices for faculty members. These offices, originally designed for two people, had been occupied by only one. As it happened, some of the humanities departments were the most favored, and usage had hallowed that arrangement. Then, as the student population expanded and the faculty grew, the pressures on space increased. The campus began to run a slight temperature on the issue. An enthusiastic dean, with two bright, young, and vigorous administrative accomplices, drew up a plan for reassigning office space more equitably. The president was assured that all parties had been consulted and that everyone had conceded the justice of the new arrangements. Indeed, they probably had in general terms. This was different, however, from saying that everyone working alone in a two-person office had agreed to share with a partner. When the proposal was presented to the campus late in the spring, to take effect in the fall, pandemonium followed.

It would have been better to announce the plan as effective three years hence, with a phasing in during that interval. Each

detail of the proposal should have been worked through in lei-
surely fashion. After all, universities stay in place for one hundred
years ("sometimes three hundred years," a New England colleague
sniffs). Two or three years' delay on issues that are not of overwhelming urgency, in order to preserve feelings of due process
and justice on the campus, is acceptable. I have observed that once
a solution has been announced to be effective in a year or two, the
disaffected resign themselves and the pressure is reduced
significantly.

Time Sensitivities. One function of administrators, at least
those with a democratic style, is to help absorb the anxiety of
others, as well as to manage their own. Insensitivity to timing can
sometimes increase the burden of anxiety for other people. An
administrator returning from a trip, for example, should bear in
mind that the campus has functioned, has been solving day-to-day
problems, in his or her absence. The administrator probably feels
a bit guilty for having gone away and may also sense a slight and
unconscious resentment among those who stayed on campus—those
remaining at work are resentful, perhaps simply because someone
else got a trip they didn't or perhaps because the missing administrator wasn't there to share the burdens of problem solving. If
an administrator returns from off-campus events and immediately
begins ordering people about or jumping into the middle of problems without taking time to be briefed, he can create problems.

Similar considerations should be observed by those remaining at work. They should resist the tendency to rush in and dump
all their worries on the "boss" the minute he gets back from a trip
or from vacation. Of course, sometimes they have to, but most of
the time, problems will wait for a few hours or even a day or two.

There is another tendency to be curbed. It's easy to develop
the habit of unloading anxieties on the boss at the end of the week
so that the weekend is psychologically clear. The difficulty, of
course, is that the other person carries the burden over the weekend with no possibility of working out the problems before operations resume on Monday.

Finally, on this theme, I have noticed that insensitivity to
time pressures can be a continuing irritant in the relations among
administrative team members. If one administrator, for example,

is working feverishly to meet a deadline, another person's coming in for a long discursive conversation is annoying. Similarly, a feeling of urgency and frenzy on the part of a colleague when working through problems can be annoying to the other partner in the discussion if he wishes to explore nuances and peripheral ramifications. Adjusting to one another's sense of time and pacing helps to build a cohesive work team.

Importance of the Calendar. I have developed an almost superstitious feeling about the calendar. It seems to me, for example, the spring is the time of bacchanalia, human sacrifice, and disaster for well-ordered social systems. It was not accidental that the great fertility festivals took place in the spring, with accompanying license and culturally approved release. In the university community, spring will be the time of major student disorders; spring will be the time of faculty heart attacks; spring will be the time when tempers are short and administrative judgment is frayed. As a colleague once remarked, "The bitch of misunderstanding is in heat."

There are additional refinements of which I am less certain. But it seems to me that everyone grows tighter and tighter as the fall semester progresses. The schedule of work compresses. The feeling of too much to do in too little time accelerates until the Christmas break. Then begins a period I think of as a "trough," when pressures ease off, the workload moderates, and cooler heads prevail. The pressure then continues to build, reaching a climax at the end of the spring semester. The last three weeks before commencement are when pandemonium breaks loose, if it is going to break loose at any time in the calendar year. Although you can't live by the calendar, letting it govern every administrative action, it pays to be aware of its relationship to campus mood.

Perceptions of the Faculty

The Abrasive Faculty. Long ago, Benjamin Franklin observed that persons of good sense seldom fall into extended disputation, with the exception of three classes of people: "lawyers, men of all sorts that had been bred in Edinburgh and university men." Deane Marlott, former president of Cornell University, expressed a harsher opinion of the Cornell faculty when he stated that "some of those brilliant minds are encased in some of the most miserable human beings on earth."

Sometimes people outside universities charge that such institutions offer shelter and high-paying positions to "kooks" who could not hold a job in any other sector of the society. When not openly stated, such views may be cherished as inner convictions. Academics are suspected and accused of being arrogant, rude, overbearing, and in all ways uncivil.

After long and intimate experience with faculties, I am convinced that such charges are overdrawn to the point of caricature. Most academics are about as civil as other highly intelligent creative people with a job to do and a conviction about the importance of that responsibility. On balance, that's usually pretty civil. It is paradoxical that the same people who have such deep faith in scientists and scholars as individuals can express such thinly veiled contempt for them when they are gathered together in a university.

Many times when I have received a complaint from someone outside the academic community about a professor's rude behavior, inquiry reveals that rudeness was present on both sides. More frequently than not, the professor was provoked by the complainer's assumption that the professor was a subordinate or employee by some influential donor or "taxpayer," and the complainer was affronted by the academic's unwillingness to accept this status. This observation, of course, does not explain every incident.

From a societal point of view, it is very difficult to determine, in the long term, who is a kook and who is not. If a university attempted to hire only polite and unabrasive people, the society would, at some point, be robbed of rich resources of talent and imagination. Creative people are not always polite people. Many are eccentric by the standards of at least some group in the community. The problem is that one man's kookiness is another man's sanity. It is important to a society, as well as to a university, to permit idiosyncrasy, short of behavior that interferes with the freedom of others.

As the example above made clear, academics don't see eye to eye with some members of the general public about what their proper role and status should be. Academics consider themselves under obligation to independence, clear-sightedness, and fearlessness in following the implications of their scholarship and their convictions. (Sometimes, of course, they overextend the franchise into a "license" for indiscriminate rudeness with expectations of impunity.) Those outside the academic community, in contrast, sometimes have the view that academics are hired hands put in universities to keep young people off the streets and creatively occupied. Professors are supposed to do what they are told. Regrettably, there is something of a double standard involved in this perception. On occasion, a public pronouncement deemed "fearless," "direct," "honest," and "well-deserved" when it comes from a captain of industry would be seen in a different light when delivered by an assistant professor of political science; from the latter, the statements might be regarded as "ungrateful," "bigoted," "self-serving," or "outrageously rude."

A fair percentage of the time, faculties gain their reputation for being uncivil not from attacks they make on the outside community but from reports in the media of statements made on campus and about university affairs. Here the public perception of faculty members as unreasonably contentious arises from a failure to appreciate the democratic and political nature and functioning of an academic community and the political role faculty members legitimately play in that process. Remarks that would be regarded as entirely proper, even though abrasive, when addressed by a legislator to his colleagues on the floor of the legislature might be regarded by the general public as unacceptable if they were delivered by a faculty member at an opening meeting of the academic senate and reported in the local press. Nevertheless, the political functioning of both bodies may be the same. Harlan Cleveland (1972, p. 39) makes the point well. "The analogy between an academic faculty and a political legislature is apt. Every faculty member is juridically free and equal—a politically acceptable (if practically unrealistic) organization chart for a university faculty could be drawn only by placing all the names in a horizontal line on a long roll of paper."

Administrators too are not immune to the stereotype of faculty members as abrasive "eccentrics." This conception is wrong not only for the reasons presented above but because it perpetuates and reinforces the notion of administrators as wiser and better equipped to decide what is good for faculty members than they are. The tone of an administrative style is distorted when this kind of assumption operates. It creates a climate in which administrative mistakes on the basis of "royalist" assumptions become more common. More than that, as pointed out elsewhere, this kind of stereotyping, not only of the faculty by the administration but the reverse as well, moves disagreements toward unreasonable and frivolous confrontations and quarrels. Fortunately, the democratic style I am discussing, which creates a climate, an atmosphere, in which misunderstandings and disagreements are perceived as part of the political dialectic, can help to prevent stereotyped splits on campus.

The notion that faculty members are sometimes unappealingly unique is taken so seriously by some that they have even suggested that the socialization of faculty members is different from that of other professionals. These writers argue that early socialization patterns predispose academics to be gifted and yet twisted at the same time and therefore to gravitate toward universities for refuge. This idea lost credibility in the sixties, when large, miscellaneous, and generally middle-class student bodies became even more outrageously uncivil than professors. Thus to the extent that faculty behavior seems unique, this uniqueness arises from the structuring of reality on campus rather than from the extrapolation of individual development curves. Abrasiveness in a university is much more comprehensible in political terms than in psychological ones.

The Impractical Faculty. Some members of the general public consider faculty members not only unpleasant but impractical. This view of academics is not new. Edmund Burke wrote in *Reflections on the Revolution in France,* "When men are too much confined to professional and faculty habits and as it were inveterate in the recurrent employment of that narrow circle, they are rather disabled than qualified for whatever depends on the knowledge of mankind, on experience in mixed affairs, on a comprehensive, connected view of the various complicated, external, and internal interests, which go to the formation of that multifarious thing called a state" (Dubos, 1974/75, p. 10). A contemporary, perhaps even more critical, observer comments, "Academic intellectuals are especially subject to emotional enthusiasms and especially insulated from the chilly effects of objective reality. It is not merely that professors have never had to meet a payroll; they have also never had to meet a scoreboard or any other crucial experiment whose outcome would determine their fate by testing how closely their ideas fit the actual reality. Academics are protected not only by tenure, but also by their own ability to rationalize, complicate and mystify. They do not like objective processes whose results cannot be talked away" (Sowell, 1975, p. 20).

In another context, a writer for the *Boston Globe,* having observed that college professors are often poor writers, continues, "They are lousy writers because their years of academic parochialism prevent them from seeing gray areas, so almost everything is nice and neat and right or wrong or good and bad. But life just doesn't work that way" (Murphy, 1974).

Every administrator and faculty member has seen evidence to support, at least to a degree, these attitudes. One piece of evidence was supplied me by the following episode.

A number of years ago on a large, battered campus of a large system, things were not going well with higher education. The governor and the legislature seemed to have joined in a concerted effort to cut back on budgets at a time when enrollment pressures on the campuses were increasing rapidly. An experienced faculty member, exceedingly bright in his academic field and with no additional symptoms of giddiness, said to me one day, speaking as a colleague and as an old friend, "Don, if things don't start getting better, the faculty may have to go on strike." I confessed to him that I received the news with some dismay and pointed out that if those were their intentions, then plans should be made to allocate reserves from the strike fund. The faculty member asked, "What strike fund?" A great suspicion dawned. "How would you live?" I asked. "You have two kids in college, you are supporting two automobiles and paying the mortgage on an expensive house." His confusion was only momentary. He replied with great guilelessness, "Why I would simply live on my salary."

This example is extreme, yet I was not kidding when I said this faculty member was a very bright man. His kind of reality problem is not psychological but structural. The problem is not that faculty members have had unique childhoods or that the more impractical and fuzzy-headed intellects of the society are attracted to faculties—I have seen no convincing evidence for the latter. The trouble is that the university is a system that actively trains for certain kinds of incapacity. Professors, like other people, develop pockets of impracticality when they are not involved in the complexities of a situation but have legitimate interests and strong feelings.

I have mentioned elsewhere the great body of research work supporting the opinion that people, when involved in fundamental ways in decisions that affect them, will indeed become highly sophisticated, responsible, and even altruistic. An illustration comes to mind. When, at one point in the history of a university, it became apparent that budgets might actually be cut to such an extent that permanent employees would be dismissed, each of the three unions serving the various personnel groups of the campus were called in for a briefing. The discussion was serious and frank. Questions were pointed and intelligent. It became apparent that the administrators were not playing games, that the threat was real. Later in the week, key representatives of each union came privately to the president and suggested that before the employees in any group, including the other unions, were laid off, the union leadership be consulted. They felt the members of their particular union would rather take voluntary cuts in pay than have anyone dismissed. Each representative was unaware that the others had come forward. Here was not only a good show of altruism but a fair demonstration of practicality and problem-solving capacity.

The Faculty and Governance. The view that faculty members are irresponsible is used to argue against the involvement of the faculty in governing the university. Professors, it is said, fail to face problems realistically or will not come to hard, realistic solutions. If left to their own devices, they are guilty of poor judgment and self-serving answers. Therefore, it is argued, any administrative style based on assumptions of faculty responsibility, maturity, and problem-solving capacity will fail. Of course the result of such prophecies is that they become self-fulfilling.

Sometimes the argument for disqualifying faculty members from involvement in decision making takes a different tack. Some people state, on the one hand, that most professors are not interested in participating in administrative processes and, on the other, that those who are interested tend to be the most irresponsible segments of the faculty. The first argument has received some support from research studies (Gross and Grambsch, 1974). But the fact that members of the faculty are not, under present conditions and as a general group, interested in administration does not mean that they are not obviously interested under certain conditions. Let some suspicion of injustice or high-handed activity on the part of administrators and trustees be brought to the attention of the faculty, and astonishing amounts of involvement take place immediately. And as for the second argument—that when faculty do become involved in governing a university, only the discontented and the least able participate—I have found it to be incorrect. In my observation, those campuses where seemingly only the hostile members of the faculty try to take part in governance are also those campuses where administration is trying with small success to keep the faculty "out of management."

Opponents of faculty participation also take still a different approach, asserting that faculty members should not be interested in administration. They should be interested only in their scholarly endeavors. Furthermore, it is contended, when universities are properly run, most faculty members do focus primarily on scholarship. Even if this view is correct, the fact that faculty members can be involved if they wish to be in administrative decisions, and are involved meaningfully to the extent that they are interested, changes the chemistry of the administrative process.

In the final analysis, the arguments against democratic participation on a university campus are the same as those used to criticize the democratic state: most people in a democracy are not continuously concerned with political activity or with the processes of government; they are not informed on the issues; their votes are based on emotions—the criticisms are legion. Who would argue successfully, however, in spite of these criticisms, that governance should be structured in such a way that the average citizen should not have the right to be involved?

In any event, the democratic political style under discussion makes it possible and more attractive for the great middle group of the faculty to participate in the affairs of the university. In this regard, I have a fantasy of how a faculty might be responsibly involved, for instance, in the fiscal decisions of a university. The scenario may have been approximated on a campus or two, but the full implications of the philosophy and the procedure that I envision have not been played out completely. Admittedly, the logistical problems would be enormous.

Budgeting is one of the most time-consuming and sometimes frustrating problems with which an administration must contend. The present problem with faculty members' involvement in the budget process is that the name of the game for them is often simply "more." Usually, neither faculty members nor department chairpersons have difficult choices to make. The heat drifts to the top. Tough decisions are made by a dean or a president or a business manager, who then takes the lashes.

Let's suppose, instead, that a representative budget committee, fully aware of all the budget circumstances of the university, were to make lump-sum formula allocations to each department. Once allocation decisions had been made creditably, the department would become a center of decision making within limits laid down for the general university. There would be a computer-assisted charge-back system for every service supplied to each department. Everything would be accounted for. Each classroom would have a price tag that would vary depending on the time of day. Prime time would be more expensive. There would be a charge for the heating and lighting. Department stationery also would have a price tag; so would telephone service, travel, equipment, professional salaries, and secretarial support. Everything would be in the computer. Suppose the department were responsible for all decisions concerning the distribution of funds, again with general guidelines deemed necessary to the welfare of the university, such as the fixing of maximum student-faculty ratios. Even decisions such as whether to hire one full professor at a top salary or two assistant professors at a median salary would be left to the department. The problem of how much to spend for telephone service would be a departmental decision, and so on.

Let's imagine a hypothetical conversation with such an arrangement in force. A department chairperson comes to see the dean.

Dean Able: Now let's see, Dr. Baker. As chairman of the department, you said you wish all thirty members of your faculty to go to the annual meeting in Hawaii.

Dr. Baker: Yes, that's right. It's most important that every member of the department have that type of professional exposure.

Dean Able: How many members of the department are reading a paper at the meetings?

Dr. Baker: Two.

Dean Able: Have you thought of the fact that you're also hoping to add two assistant professors to the department for next fall? If you were to send to Hawaii only those two members of the department who are reading papers, because of the great distance involved, you would save enough money to almost pay the salary of one assistant professor.

Dr. Baker: Is that right? I hadn't realized it would cost so much. Where can I get a breakdown on that kind of information?

Dean Able: From the computer center. There's a fiscal advisor assigned to every department who can give you computer breakouts on the costs of each item in the budget. You can also compare the percentages that you're spending with the spending patterns of other departments.

Dr. Baker: Yes, I've heard about that. That sort of information would be helpful. Perhaps you're right about the annual meeting.

Dean Able: I notice you're also requesting two additional secretaries for the department. Have you thought about cutting down on the number of classrooms you're asking for? I see that the schedule you submitted calls for all your classes to be held between nine and two on Monday, Wednesday, and Friday.

Dr. Baker: Yes. Those are the teaching preferences of our faculty.

Dean Able: I'm certain you're aware that we have to charge premium rates for the use of rooms at prime time because the demand is so great. If you were to use 30 percent fewer rooms, you could still accommodate all your classes by running from eight in the morning until five in the afternoon. The charge for the early morning and afternoon hours is negligible compared with the cost of prime time. If you spread your classes over a longer day and more days of the week, you'd have enough money left for at least one of those secretaries.

Dr. Baker: I believe the department would go for that if they understood what the choices were.

Dean Able: You've asked for a phone with two or three outside lines and a phone monitor for every member of the faculty. Now let me show you how much money you would save if. . . .

You can finish the rest of the conversation yourself. The point is that faculty members can and do make responsible decisions when they regard the rules as fair and the decisions as critical, when the choices are meaningful and the guidelines comprehensible. Don't give me any garbage about faculty members being some kind of unique creatures less susceptible to reasonable behavior than lawyers or whatever reference group you care to enter into the discussion. I don't believe it.

I've had objections to such democratic proposals from presidents who complain of the tendency of faculty members, in choosing their colleagues, to "hire trouble makers." Presidents assert that every time hiring choices are left to the department, people are proposed for appointment who seem to have very little to recommend them except a record of campus and political agitation about issues outside their field of expertise. Lacking any other model to explain the phenomenon, the presidents are reduced to the "impractical" stereotype.

Such behavior is readily comprehensible under the political model. When faculty members feel on the short end of the power teeter-totter, they present recommendations to redress the balance. In my experience, where an administrative group is "uptight" about getting "good" faculty members, and when *good* means faculty members who are thoroughly tame, the pressure in the opposite direction becomes great. In contrast, I have noticed a sharp decline in the tendency to pick academic colleagues on grounds other than competence when faculty members are genuinely involved in the governance of the institution and in personnel decisions. This is not to say that there cannot be very competent people who are also abrasive.

To Fire or Not to Fire. Many university presidents fantasize about the therapeutic effects on the institution of extracting six or seven of the sore teeth faculty. The fantasy arises from a lack of perceptiveness about or experience with the way universities actually operate. I am impressed with the fact that the same types of dissidents exist on every campus. Only their names and their departments vary. More than that, I am convinced that when one disappears, another springs up as a replacement. The democratic political model of the university makes this phenomenon understandable and acceptable. Remember that dissent is legitimate and it is healthy. The individuals involved only illustrate the process. They do not create it. In fact, as I've said before, such opposition figures play a useful and even essential role. Nevertheless, on a healthy campus they will not dominate. The influence that intemperate opinion leaders will have is a fairly rough index of morale and spirit on the campus. The better the morale, the lower the influence.

Since dissent is natural and desirable, attempting to solve campus problems by dismissals is counterproductive. Such a strategy is also inadequate for other reasons. To repeat, a person's strengths are frequently also that person's weaknesses. Every virtue has its attendant flaw. Sometimes that flaw is merely a matter of the application of the virtue. If an administrator, for example, creates problems because of teutonic and aggressive ways, he or she will, nevertheless, be a tower of strength when an aggressive style is needed in a particular situation. A literal fiscal type, who drives his colleagues crazy by punctilious interpretations of formulas and endless quibbles about the balance sheet, may on occasion be one of the most useful members of the team. The primary responsibility of administration may not be to get rid of "incompetents," a small, even mythical group on most university campuses, but rather to see, with an eye to minimizing their weaknesses, that the skills of people are related to the needs of the organization.

Another difficulty with the firing strategy is that firing spreads. A president who has finally agreed to remove (rather than try to repair) one troublesome dean calls the person in and pulls the pin. He is surprised to be confronted in the following few weeks with demands for the dismissal or reassignment of a dozen other administrators. In certain diseased instances the plea can become "just twelve more therapeutic murders and this place will be all right." The solving-by-elimination strategy carries in it the seeds of an unreal notion of problems. Most problems are truly not created by "bad" people.

Footnotes on Human Relations

An improvement in circumstance does not always improve feelings. These days we frequently hear references to the "revolution of rising expectations." The insight behind the phrase goes back at least to deTocqueville. I remember how surprised I was to learn in an undergraduate history class that one of the probable causes of the French Revolution was the rapid improvement in the condition of the French peasantry. The professor confided that, at the time, the circumstances of the dispossessed in France had improved more rapidly than those in any other country in Europe.

The Protestant ethic predisposes administrators to attitudinal biases that are difficult to surmount. We are conditioned to see the world operating as a series of small dramas in which good performance is successful and rewarded. As administrators, we do a good job; we solve problems. We make things better, and presto, everyone is happier. This scenario is unrealistic. On the contrary, it seems that we can often anticipate the greatest unhappiness over space assignments the year that two new buildings are opened on campus and there is more room for everyone. Seasoned administrators have ceased to be astonished when the largest increase in salaries in three years gives rise to the most continuous and unhappy discussions about comparative salaries. One college president, deeply concerned with the rights of women, pushed hard for the establishment of a women's studies program. Some months later, he complained rather bitterly, "I've done more than anyone within a thousand-mile radius to establish the principle of equal rights for women, and I'm the only one that's being sued by every woman in sight."

Another illustration comes to mind. A young president who had just assumed office received several complaints that his predecessor had not communicated effectively with the faculty. To improve the situation, he scheduled a series of bull sessions with small groups of faculty members in his home. At first, the informal gatherings produced high morale. Word began to spread that "the president cares." But the change in mood was relatively short-lived. Those who had not yet been invited to the president's home became even more vocal in their discontent. Those who had participated began to complain that all the president did was just to listen and that things were moving too slowly. The comments became more numerous to the effect that the president should not spend all his time listening to soreheads.

A more general application of the fact that criticism often follows improvement is found in the arena of affirmative-action compliance, a critical one for the society and for universities generally. The schools that seemed to be "catching it" from enforcement agencies, at least in the early days, were often not traditional, diehard, truly resistant universities but campuses that had obviously been making serious efforts to establish good affirmative-action records.

The implication for administrative style of all these observations is not that cynicism is reality training but that the most successful executives are not the hard-headed, "fact" administrators; they are those who deal with the world as people perceive it to be rather than as they themselves believe it is or ought to be. Understanding the way the administrative world actually is—with few self-evident facts and many legitimate interpretations—creates better problem solving and more forward movement in an institution. When they see this, administrators are not so easily sidetracked by continual gloomy post-mortems or so likely to mutter about ungrateful or perverse faculty members, students, and trustees.

Battle Seldom Won or Lost. The concept of campus problems that administrators have in their heads obviously has immense importance in determining administrative strategies. If they view criticisms and other problems as cause for war, with tactical positions to be gained or sacrificed, their style has one tone. But if they see difficulties as part of a continuous dialectic of change which gives institutions and individuals opportunities to grow, the texturing of the situation is quite different.

Under the combat model, stories of administrative struggles repeated to fellow administrators usually end like a drama with the battle either won or lost, but certainly over. In my experience, the real administrative world doesn't operate in that fashion. In the academy, battles are never won as decisively as they sometimes appear to be. Many an administrator, feeling that a struggle has been successfully concluded and that he or she has "won" hands down—no hard feelings—finds that those who have "lost" join others in a coalition of the "defeated" to pick up the struggle on a new issue. Personnel cases, for example, seem never to go away. They enter the germ plasm of an institution and give rise to mutations forever.

In periods where things are going well, it is easy for a president or dean to imagine that one or more struggles have subsided, that his opponents have now either become neutral or supportive. This notion is frequently an illusion. Under a dialectic model, one does not hunt for signs of closure in the same sense. There is a feeling of process and growth rather than of wins and losses.

Not Just for Convenience. If the rationale for an action is just administrative convenience, don't do it. An illustration: The bookstore has pursued a policy of extending credit to students and faculty members. Suddenly the bookstore manager brings information to the administrative team that the bookstore is several thousand dollars in debt as a result of the policy. Those who have been extended credit simply have not paid. In the course of the staff discussion of the problem, the first proposal is to eliminate all credit for everyone. After careful analysis, the staff determines that the only real justification for an apocalyptic change in policy would be administrative convenience.

Since that rationale is not sufficient, they break down the problem. A brief analysis of material at hand indicates that groups, under one or another state- or institutionally sponsored program, are not a problem, because a claim can be made to the funding agency in case of default, if the credit has been offered with their approval. But 90 percent of the loss has been created by students with no guarantors. They have simply not paid their debts. Sometimes faculty members are also at fault. They ask for free advance copies of texts on the pledge that they will write to publishers and turn over the company copies to the bookstore. The bookstore never receives the promised volumes.

As a consequence of this analysis, several new arrangements are made. Faculty members pay for their examination copies. They are reimbursed for the cost when the books from the publisher are turned in to the bookstore. Individual cases of bookstore debt are handled through personal interviews, and additional credit is denied until the debt is paid. The end result is that, instead of overcorrecting the compass in the interest of administrative convenience, or the relief of anxiety, the bookstore makes a series of differentiated judgments in granting loans. If one views the university as a democratic political community, it should be obvious that administration is not an end in itself, yet to act primarily in the interest of administrative convenience is to treat it as such.

Eight

———✦———

Answers to
Common Anxieties

I speak of anxieties about the style rather than problems with the style for two reasons. First, there is not enough documented experience with this or similar styles to really be certain what the problems are. Administrators operating under related cosmologies have not identified them with coherent styles.

This is not to deny that difficulties exist. There are problems with any style or philosophy. But the person who hunts for perfect and final solutions is doomed. Many of the problems within organizations that cry for solution today were once introduced as solutions to previous pressing concerns. Every solution to a problem in turn becomes a problem of its own, generating its own tensions, frustrations, and unfulfilled expectations. The "solution-now-become-problem" is answered by another solution which in turn becomes problem. It is a process world.

The second reason that the term *anxieties* may be more appropriate than problems is more complex. How does one separate the philosophy under which any organization is administered from the practice of the philosophy? The theory and perspective may be better than the application of the art. Or, conversely, a skillful practitioner may parlay crippled theory into Olympic performance. The problems with the style, therefore, translate largely into anxieties and concerns about the philosophy, perhaps also informed by cynicisms developed from experience. For example: "I once tried getting the faculty involved in a critical decision, and they threw up on me. They simply looked at the problem, debated it, then pushed it back across my desk in worse shape than before. Nobody else would make the decision or even help."

The point bears reemphasis that administrators hold in their psyches an intuitive metaphysic about people. They have a predisposition to believe, for example, that either people can be trusted or they can't. If the deep suspicion is that, indeed, people cannot be trusted, then whatever answers I give here will be at best temporarily reassuring. Any example of acceptable results achieved under the style of operation that forms the subject of this volume will be shrugged off as fortunate fluke, and, of course, in all honesty, for most of us the universe comes without guarantees and with certitude rather than certainty. Such critics may be right. Still, I have found the opposite to be true. With appropriate perceptions, definitions, and structures to guide their interactions, people can be trusted.

In general, the anxieties created in administrators by democratic political styles are the same kinds of difficulties experienced by leaders in the democratic political state. I believe it was Ortega y Gasset who once remarked that an authoritarian state is like a magnificent galleon with all sails set—beautiful to behold. The difficulty is that when the galleon hits a rock, it sinks to the bottom. Democracy, in contrast, is like a raft. It never sinks but your feet are always wet.

In the remainder of this chapter, I will present anxieties about getting wet feet and other matters in the form of typical questions.

What happens when appropriate groups participating in a decision-

making process simply refuse to make a decision? The specter of the resistant, impractical, and hostile faculty refusing to take its share of
responsibility is indeed the ghost that pursues us in a democratic
political style, just as in more traditional styles the ultimate anxiety
that skulks is the fear that the "troops" will not obey orders. What
is to be done in case of mutiny? There is evidence close at hand,
and from everyday experience, of people refusing to take responsibility. "That's not the job of the faculty. That's the job of the
administration. You are paid to make the tough decisions!" There
is a measure of truth in such assertions, of course. Administrators
should not use the existence of a participative style of decision
making as an excuse to evade responsibility themselves. Administrators should not use democratic devices to escape criticism. That's
not the point of the style. The aim is to get better decisions, more
effectively made.

Nevertheless, because the threat that the faculty and sometimes the student body will refuse to take responsibility under the
style I am talking about seems more real than the threat of mutiny
under traditional styles, we are more quickly tempted to surrender
the battle, throw up our hands, and fall back on problem solving
from the top down? Again, I am not saying that occasionally it
doesn't have to be done, or that sometimes it may not be the best
thing for all concerned. I am just saying that we usually give up
too soon and frequently get results that are not as satisfactory as
those derived from team problem solving and consensus building.

But what of the ultimate catastrophe, the faculty refuses to
help with a tough problem? When this occurs, I think that frequently what has taken place is that the faculty has given consent
without approval. They intuitively recognize that there are no good
answers and that someone must simply take the heat. Administrative decision under these circumstances will, in my experience, lead
only to grumbling and not to revolution among the faculty. And
thus what appears a catastrophe is often an arrangement administrators can live with. Pushing all responsibility on the administration may also have just a slight flavor of testing the system and
perhaps also giving the administration a rough time. All of this is
normal. Proceed and be of good heart.

Of course, if such incidents become chronic, the possibility should be considered that the power of the administrator as an effective democratic political leader is on the decline. It may be time for a change.

What happens when everyone is accustomed to a participative, democratic style and problems come along that cannot be solved by participation and team effort, such as a budget cut by the legislature in a public institution? In the real world of administration, the major difficulty is to get large numbers of people to completely understand the critical nature of an urgent problem. It is unlikely that participation and the demand for greater participation will create problems. Indeed, the demand for participation in problem solving and decision making can only help. Without the cooperation of faculty members and sometimes students, there simply are no solutions for the problems created, for example, by a major budget cut involving personnel layoffs. Budget cuts are tough in any event. If there is a tradition on the campus of team problem solving and a resulting feeling of "we" in owning the problem, the chances of arriving at a least-cost adjustment to the situation are probably better.

Remember, however, several years of concatenated budget disaster mean trouble for every administrator. That fact might as well be recognized and accepted. An early warning system for hurricanes and storm shelters still does not guarantee happy victims.

Isn't it true that people take advantage of democratic political styles of administration and "goof off"? A fellow administrator of experience and wisdom once commented, "the trouble with hard-jawed, down-from-the-top administration is that after a while everyone spends a lot of time trying to beat the system. Nobody works unless hard eyes are on him, and he's really 'under the gun.' The trouble with a system that is more humanly oriented is that after a while nobody comes to work." The comment reflects the stereotype that democratic styles lead people to take advantage of the system. This is probably true if such styles are equated with a laissez-faire model in which everyone simply moves in his own random orbit. But in my experience democratic styles can be very demanding, with high expectations and therefore people tend to impose high expectations on themselves, working more, not less.

If a team member is or appears to be taking advantage,

there isn't a thing in this style that prohibits an administrator from saying to the person, for instance, "A lot of people are watching us. Let's not be too relaxed. The fact that you're coming in at nine-thirty every day is giving the wrong signal to some. How would you feel about being here by eight?" If there are reasons for the late arrival of which the administrator making the presentation is unaware, such as the fact that the person involved has been working until one every morning for three weeks getting out a special assignment, then a lot of time isn't wasted mending injured feelings.

Again, it's very easy to forget that most people obey the law not because there are policemen around to make them do so but because most of the time they want to behave properly and because it is habitual to do so. If this were not the case, there simply aren't enough policemen in the world to catch every wrongdoer. Consequently, on a university campus where there is much wit and wisdom aggregated, if the name of the game becomes "beat the system," watch out! The budget simply won't stand the cost of a police system to manage things.

Under democratic political styles, don't large campus groups override and exploit smaller groups? It is true that before a university commits itself to a course of action, proposals must be tested in a climate of majority opinion. However, these styles strongly emphasize guarantees against the infringement of the rights of individuals. In addition, small groups rapidly learn the value of coalition and compromise.

Finally, I think it is fair to say that under the style here outlined, the level of mutual respect and tolerance can be higher than that under traditional styles. Instances of majority groups exploiting smaller groups or overriding them in a ruthless way are rare in my observation.

Isn't there a danger that the democratic political style will make possible a tyranny of the minority? The chances of minority opinion prevailing over the will of the majority are probably less in the style discussed in this book than under more traditional styles of university administration. Under more traditional arrangements, it's very difficult for top management to judge the representative strength of different groups. Bear in mind that the system we are discussing emphatically does not operate on the premise that all opinions are equal. But it is based on democratically developed procedures. Under good circumstances, therefore, evaluating the true character of majority opinion should be easier.

Again bear in mind that this style does not mean that every item of university business is a matter for faculty and student decision or vote. In general, the authority to make decisions rests with groups to the degree that they will be affected by those decisions. Major responsibility for some decisions lies properly with the administration. The notion that ultimately such democratic ideals will lead to the demand that everything be decided by the "mob in the quad" simply is not supported by practical experience.

Doesn't the style tend to develop factions within an academic community? This anxiety about democratic political systems goes back at least to James Madison, who complained that popular governments had a tendency to develop factions which produced "instability, injustice and confusion" (Ranney and Kindall, 1956, p. 132).

One of the principal assets of a democratic system, in my view, is its ability to use miscellaneity as a strength. There will always be factions among people. Differences will find expression, openly under democratic and free systems, covertly under repressive systems. Democracy, politics, and participation do not create factions, they permit them to surface and to function. The trick, of course, is to find ways of using them in dialectic change strategies and melding them into compromise, wider consensus, and adaptive synthesis.

Isn't it true that any administrative style, including this one, will be understood by and limited in its intimate effects to the members of a tight team? Isn't it true, then, that even in moderately large institutions the "provinces" never get the word? Most of the faculty won't read the president's speeches, many will not go to faculty meetings, most will not be involved intimately in the administrative machinery of the institution. So it's undoubtedly true that not everyone in an institution, including a small institution, "gets the word" on schedule. The word seems eventually to get around, however. The freedom to disagree, the extreme emphasis on channels, the hospitable reception of dissenting opinion, the absence of royalist pronouncements and patrician egos in key members of the team, the stress on problem solving rather than on the exercise of authority, the concern with fairness, which, when it is communicated from the top, in a very real sense coerces everyone to subscribe to the cosmology—all these things eventually are communicated through organizations of any size.

In a more direct fashion, faculty members are affected by tidy, fair, and impartial grievance procedures, open elections, and the other apparatuses of a democratic political system. They have at least a feeling that they know how the rules are made and what general procedures have been set up to redress injustice or attend to grievance.

Doesn't the style create problems when it succeeds? Doesn't participation generate the need for more? In my experience, participation does not automatically result in ever-increasing participation. It creates the expectation and demand for the *possibility* of more participation. When people want to join in solving the problem, I say, "Let them in." It's always possible to avoid unworkable and single-minded ideological solutions by being certain that the committee, task force, or whatever appropriate group addresses the problem is broadly representative. In my experience democratic political administrative styles make that easier to arrange than do traditional styles. Sometimes, after faculty members and students discover that participation is an honest and consistent agenda item, the problem may become just the opposite. Considerable effort may be required on a continuing basis to keep the level of involvement high, even on critical issues.

Axioms for Effective Administrators

According to legend, at the request of a dying king, the Royal Council of Sages once capsulized all wisdom in a single word—*perhaps*. For the effective college or university administrator, however, one such word of wisdom will hardly suffice. At least three general propositions, I would urge, deserve special attention:

- Respect the people with whom you work.
- Understand the university for which you work.
- Remember, as an administrator, why you are there.

Even these admonitions, despite their basic worth, may seem way too broad or lofty. For colleagues seeking practical advice for the everyday realities of their jobs, I offer the following observations or "axioms." Unfortunately, these reminders for effective administration, while more specific, do not fall into neat categories but frequently overlap and blend together:

- The university is filled with talented, sensitive human beings. Don't forget it. It is too easy to assume that people beneath you in the administrative structure are beneath you in other ways too.
- The job of administration is to call forth talent—to help people work in effective and constructive ways. Health and vitality come from the bottom up and one should take care not to stifle the sources of creativity.
- Those closest to the problem often have the best solutions. Consult them first.
- When problems become complicated, shorten the administrative lines. Get everyone concerned in the same room.
- An administrator works with the consent of the governed. The most reliable tools of the administrator are diplomacy and persuasion.
- Learn the values of persistence and patience. Too often administrators give up too soon.
- Don't underestimate the strength of a team. It is true—all of us together are smarter than any of us alone.
- Credit can and should be widely shared. Such sharing does not diminish individual accolades.
- The best administration proceeds on the assumption of health in the organization, rather than disease. Too often, pathological explanations of campus events reveal the absence of realistic views of how the organization actually works.
- The most important administrative task is not police duty but problem solving. The most important question is not who is responsible for our "mistakes" but "how do we get better solutions for the problems before us?"
- The university is active and reactive. Understand the way it behaves and work *with* it, not against it.

- The secret cement of any organization is trust. Almost anything will work when enough trust is present. Without it, nothing works.
- Use the established channels for action. Haphazard approaches to problem solving breed confusion. Consistency is a form of integrity.
- Have a sense of direction even if it's necessary to change it frequently. Keep moving. The administrator's job is proactive.
- Don't become irrevocably committed to any single solution. There are many paths to the top of the hill.
- Don't try to keep secrets. Communicate, communicate, communicate. Problems are caused by what people *don't* know.
- When you're wrong, admit it. Almost everyone will know it anyway. Your capitulation will be seen as reasonableness, not weakness.
- Don't fight imaginary wars. Comic opera struggles over symbolic issues waste everyone's time.
- Get help from everyone, but ultimately trust yourself. Have the courage to make your own mistakes and to choose your own battles.
- Don't bully, threaten, or try to get even. Remember the words of Woody Allen: "You can never get even with the world; it takes too long and too many lawyers."
- Avoid cynicism and self-pity. Don't forget, you asked for the job.
- Be optimistic. It is not that pessimism is unjustified, but it will not sustain you or your institution.
- Don't stay too long. Survivors pay too high a price personally and exact too high a price from the university. Administrators are expendable.
- Make your plans for retreat from an administrative position in advance—if possible, when you sign on. A request for tenured professorship might be considered reasonable at the time of appointment, yet it could be perceived as a demand for special privilege at the time of resignation.
- Learn to accept and use criticism, even when it makes a hard pillow.
- Be fair. Don't choose sides. Don't have pets or villains.
- Help others along the way.

References

Aleshire, F., and Aleshire, F. "Spirit of '76." *Public Administration Review,* 1976, *36* (3), 310–314.

Allison, G. "Conceptual Models in the Cuban Missile Crisis." *American Political Science Review,* 1969, *63* (3), 698–718.

Argyris, C. "How Tomorrow's Executive Will Make Decisions." *Think Magazine,* Nov./Dec. 1966, pp. 18–23.

Baldridge, J. V. *Power and Conflict in the University: Research in the Sociology of Complex Organizations.* New York: Wiley, 1971.

Bell, D. "By Whose Right?" In H. L. Hodgkinson and R. L. Meeth (Eds.), *Power and Authority: Transformation of Campus Governance.* San Francisco: Jossey-Bass, 1971.

Bell, D. "The End of Scarcity." *Saturday Review of the Society,* May 1973, pp. 49–51.

Bennis, W. "The University Leader." *Saturday Review,* December 9, 1972, pp. 42–50.

Bennis, W. "View from the Top." *Cincinnati Horizons* (published by the University of Cincinnati), April 1973, pp. 17–21.

Berger, P. L., and Luckmann, T. *The Social Construction of Reality:*

A Treatise in the Sociology of Knowledge. New York: Doubleday, 1966.

Blumstein, A., and Cohen, A. "A Theory of Punishment Stability." *Journal of Criminal Law and Criminology*, 1973, *64* (2), 198–207.

Bonham, G. W. "Who Runs the Show?" In *The Third Century: Twenty-Six Prominent Americans Speculate on the Educational Future*. New York: Change Magazine Press, 1977.

Burns, J. M. *Roosevelt: The Soldier of Freedom 1940–1945*. New York: Harcourt Brace Jovanovich, 1970.

"The Carbondale Disease." *Change*, May 1974, p. 11.

Carnegie Commission on Higher Education, The. *Governance of Higher Education: Six Priority Problems*. New York: McGraw-Hill, 1973.

Chesteron, G. K. *Orthodoxy*. New York: John Lane, 1909.

Clark, B. R. "Belief and Loyalty in College Organization." *Journal of Higher Education*, 1971, *42* (6), 499–515.

Cleveland, H. *The Future Executive*. New York: Harper & Row, 1972.

Cohen, M. D., and March, J. G. *Leadership and Ambiguity: The American College President*. New York: McGraw-Hill, 1974.

Cook, J. *In Defense of Homo Sapiens*. New York: Farrar, Straus & Giroux, 1975.

Cornuelle, R. *De-Managing America: The Final Revolution*. New York: Random House, 1975.

Cousins, N. "The Serendipitous Arena." *Saturday Review*, January 10, 1970, p. 4.

Daniels, J. *Frontiers on the Potomac*. New York: Macmillan, 1946.

Davis, W. E. "Dear Professor DeLaporte. . . ." *Chronicle of Higher Education*, November 11, 1974, p. 24.

Dubos, R. "The Despairing Optimist." *American Scholar*, Winter 1974/75, pp. 8–13.

Dumke, G. S. "Accountability and Action." Paper presented at the 13th annual meeting of the American Association of State Colleges and Universities, San Diego, Calif., November 1973.

Eliot, C. W. *The University Administrator*. Cambridge: Riverside Press, 1908.

Enarson, N. L. "The Occasional Search for the Public Interest."

Reports (published by the Association of Governing Boards of Universities and Colleges), 1975, *17* (5), 25.

Ephron, N. "The Bennington Affair." *Esquire,* September 1976, p. 58.

Fulbright, W. J. "What Is the National Interest?" *The Center Magazine,* 1974, *7* (1), 47.

Gardner, J. W. *Excellence: Can We Be Equal and Excellent Too?* New York: Harper & Row, 1961.

Gardner, J. W. "The Anti-Leadership Vaccine." In *Annual Report of the Carnegie Corporation of New York.* New York: Carnegie Corporation, 1965.

Gross, E., and Grambsch, P. V. *Changes in University Organization 1964–1971.* Report prepared for the Carnegie Commission on Higher Education. New York: McGraw-Hill, 1974.

Harper, W. R. "The College President." In *The William Rainey Harper Memorial Conference.* Chicago: University of Chicago Press, 1938.

Healy, T. J. "Anarchy and a Built-in Gyro." *Reports* (published by the Association of Governing Boards of Universities and Colleges), 1978, *20* (3), 5–13.

Hechinger, F. M. "Loss of Tenure: Return of a Nightmare." Education Section, *Saturday Review,* May 21, 1975, p. 50.

Hesburgh, T. "Letter to the Editor." *Time,* September 16, 1974, p. 36.

Hoffer, E. *The True Believer.* New York: Harper & Row, 1951.

Hutchins, R. M. "The Administrator Reconsidered: University and Foundation." In A. A. Cohen (Ed.), *Freedom, Education, and the Fund: Essays and Addresses, 1946–1956.* New York: Meridian Books, 1956.

Hutchins, R. M. "On Political Maturity." *Change,* November 1974, pp. 32–33.

"The Hutchins View of the University." *Chronicle of Higher Education,* May 23, 1977, p. 5.

Ikenberry, S. O. *The Changing Role of the College Presidency: Essays on Governance.* Washington, D.C.: American Association of State Colleges and Universities, 1974.

"In Quest of Leadership." *Time,* July 15, 1974, p. 35.

James, W. *The Will to Believe and Other Essays on Popular Philosophies.* New York: Dover, 1956. (Originally published 1897.)

Jefferson, T. *Writings of Thomas Jefferson.* (A. E. Bergh, Ed.) Washington, D. C.: Thomas Jefferson Memorial Association, 1907.

Jones, J., and Edwards, A. *Fifty Billion Dollars.* New York: Macmillan, 1951.

Kaufman, J. F. "The New College President—Expectations and Realities." *Educational Record,* Spring 1977, pp. 146–168.

Kerr, C. *The Uses of the University.* Cambridge: Harvard University Press, 1963.

Knight, E. W. *What College Presidents Say.* Chapel Hill: University of North Carolina Press, 1940.

Lahti, R. E. *Innovative College Management: Implementing Proven Organizational Practice.* San Francisco, Jossey-Bass, 1973.

Lasswell, H. D. *Politics: Who Gets What, When, How.* London: Peter Smith, 1950.

Levine, R. J. "The Outlook: Review of Current Trends in Business and Finance." *Wall Street Journal,* August 15, 1977, p. 1.

Lindblom, C. E. *The Policy-Making Process.* Englewood Cliffs, N.J.: Prentice-Hall, 1968.

Lippmann, W. "Man Must Serve Truth, Not Opinion, to Achieve Greatness." *Providence Journal,* December 16, 1974, p. A-12. (Reprinted by James Reston.)

Lowell, A. L. *What a University President Has Learned.* New York: Macmillan, 1938.

Lundborg, L. Editorial. *Los Angeles Times,* June 21, 1970, p. 3.

McGill, M. E., and Wooten, L. M. "A Symposium: Management in the Third Sector." *Public Administration Review,* 1975, *35* (5), 443–455.

McGrath, E. J. "The President as Innovator." *Selected Issues in College Administration.* New York: Teachers College Press, 1967.

Marshall, M. S. "Those Administrators." *Phi Kappa Phi Journal,* Spring 1977, pp. 10–13.

Mathews, D., and Heard, A. "Two Bicentennial Reflections for College and University Presidents." Southern University Conference, Williamsburg, Va. 1976. (No page numbers used in document.)

Merton, A. "Big Bad John." *Boston Magazine,* May 1977, p. 73.

"Middle Managers Are Disgruntled." *New Bedford Standard Times,* May 1, 1977, p. 26.

Miles, R. E. "The Pathology of Institutional Breakdown." *Journal of Higher Education,* 1969, *40* (5), 351–368.

Miller, M. *Plain Speaking: An Oral Biography of Harry Truman.* New York: Putnam, 1974.

Millett, J. *Strengthening Community in Higher Education.* Washington, D. C.: Academy for Educational Development, 1974.

Murphy, J. "The Liberals and Busing." *Boston Globe,* June 10, 1974, p. 211.

Nevins, A. *The Origins of the Land-Grant Colleges and State Universities; A Brief Account of the Morrill Act of 1862 and Its Results.* Washington, D. C.: Civil War Centennial Commission, 1962.

Oracle (University of South Florida), July 18, 1977, p. 1.

Ostrom, V. *The Intellectual Crisis in American Public Administration.* University, Ala.: University of Alabama Press, 1973.

Parker, G. T. "While Alma Mater Burns." *Atlantic Monthly,* September 1976, p. 47.

Perrow, C. B. *Organizational Analysis: A Sociological View.* Monterey, Calif.: Brooks/Cole, 1970.

Peter, L. J., and Hull, R. *The Peter Principle.* New York: William Morrow, 1976.

"Pitt Reinstates Marxist Sociologist." *Chronicle of Higher Education,* May 23, 1977, p. 3.

Ranney, A., and Kindall, W. *Democracy in the American Party System.* New York: Harcourt Brace Jovanovich, 1956.

Rehfuss, J. *Public Administration as a Political Process.* New York: Scribner's, 1973.

Reif, R. "Where Are the Leaders in Higher Education?" *Chronicle of Higher Education,* February 28, 1977, p. 32.

Review of Ephron's article on Bennington College in the September 1976 *Esquire. Time,* August 30, 1976, p. 74.

Richardson, R. D., Jr. "Staff Development: A Conceptual Framework." *Journal of Higher Education,* 1975, *46* (1), 303–311.

Sale, J. K. "Men of Low Profile." *Change,* July/August 1970, pp. 35–36.

Schlesinger, A. M., Jr. *The Coming of the New Deal*. Boston: Houghton Mifflin, 1958.

Schlesinger, A. M., Jr. *A Thousand Days*. Boston: Houghton Mifflin, 1965.

Schultze, C. L. Testimony before the subcommittee on executive reorganization of the Senate Committee on Government Operations. Washington, D. C., June 29, 1967.

Scott, A. "Management as a Political Process: Overt Versus Covert." Paper presented at the 57th annual meeting of the American Council on Education, San Diego, Calif., October, 1974.

Scott, W. "Personality Parade." *Parade*, July 14, 1974, p. 2.

A Short History of Goat Island in Newport. Newport, R. I.: Sheraton-Islander Inn, n.d.

Sowell, T. "The Intellect of the Intellectuals." *Chronicle of Higher Education*, December 8, 1975, p. 20.

Stoke, H. W. *The American College President*. New York: Harper & Row, 1959.

Thomas, L. *Lives of a Cell: Notes of a Biology Watcher*. New York: Viking Press, 1974.

Time, "On the Record," May 29, 1978, p. 85.

Tuchman, B. *The Proud Tower*. New York: Macmillan, 1966.

"200 Faces for the Future." *Time*, July 15, 1974, p. 35.

Van Dyne, L. "Ruckus in Dowagiac." *Chronicle of Higher Education*, August 19, 1974, p. 4.

Walker, D. E. "When the Tough Get Going, the Going Gets Tough: The Myth of Muscle Administration." *Public Administration Review*, 1976, *36* (4), 439–445.

Walker, D. E. Address to the Presidents' Institute, American Council on Education, June 24, 1977a, Palm Beach, Fla.

Walker, D. E. "The Contract as Constitution." Unpublished manuscript, Southeastern Massachusetts University, 1977b.

Walker, D. E. "Goodbye Mr. President and Good Luck: An Alternate Interpretation of Presidential Exit." *Educational Record*, 1977c, *58* (1), 53–58.

Walker, D. E. "Metabolic Administration." Unpublished manuscript, Southeastern Massachusetts University, 1977d.

Walker, D. E. "New Policies for Changing Institutions." In R. W.

Heyns (Ed.), *Leadership for Higher Education: A Campus View.* Washington, D. C.: American Council on Education, 1977e.

Walker, D. E., and Peiffer, H. C. "Description, Not Evaluation: Logical Confusion in Counseling." *Journal of Counseling Psychology,* 1957, *4* (2), 111–112.

Walker, D. E., Feldman, D., and Stone, G. "Collegiality and Collective Bargaining: An Alternative Perspective." *Educational Record,* Spring 1976, pp. 119–124.

Walker, D. E., Feldman, D., and Stone, G. "Achieving Institutional Goals Through Collective Bargaining." In G. W. Angell and E. P. Kelley, Jr., and Associates (Eds.), *Handbook of Faculty Bargaining: Asserting Administrative Leadership for Institutional Progress by Preparing for Bargaining, Negotiating and Administering Contracts, and Improving the Bargaining Process.* San Francisco: Jossey-Bass, 1977.

Weidlein, E. R. "True Fiction at Bennington." *Chronicle of Higher Education,* September 13, 1976, p. 16.

Wheeler, J. H. *Democracy in a Revolutionary Era: The Political Order Today.* Occasional paper *111* (2). Santa Barbara, Calif.: Center for the Study of Democratic Institutions, 1970.

Wriston, H. *The Academic Procession.* New York: Columbia University Press, 1959.

Index

203

DATE DUE

A 08 '82	
II 03 '83	

BRODART, INC.   Cat. No. 23-221